Advance Praise for *A Manager's Guide to Virtual Teams*

"The timing of this book is incredibly serendipitous, as Save the Children is making strategic changes that will rely even more on virtual teams. The book spoke to me, as it aligned with my own experience, and has become a must-read for our senior management team."

—**Justin Birtwell,** Director,
Global Learning & Development, Save the Children

"Yael has a talent for simplifying and communicating the essentials for both managers and peers in a virtual team environment. Her chapter on the importance of both nonverbal and contextual communication is critical reading for anyone who works with anyone else that is more than five meters away. Read this book and share with your team openly—but only if you want to have a well oiled virtual team."

—**Jason Madhosingh,** Director,
Online and Mobile, American Express

"Virtual teams are increasingly important in today's global economy. In *A Manager's Guide to Virtual Teams* Yael Zofi provides great commonsense advice on leading virtual teams. This book is a must-read for anyone who leads—or participates in—geographically dispersed teams."

—**Bud Bilanich,** The Common Sense Guy;
author of *Common Sense Ideas for Building a Dream Team*

"This is a 'cookbook' for successfully running a virtual team. Zofi has clearly documented the most common problems I come across, and offers pragmatic, step-by-step solutions for dealing with them. Today alone I have lived three examples from the book, and it's only 2:00 p.m. One problem dealt with remote trust and accountability; one dealt with project deliverables; and the third was a cross-cultural issue with my team in Europe, Asia, and the U.S."

—**Charles J. Rothschild,** Manager, World-Wide System Architecture,
CommTest Solutions Division, JDSU

"In her new book, *A Manager's Guide to Virtual Teams,* Yael Zofi provides a language for understanding the dynamics of virtual teams and gives insights that demystify the complexities of working across boundaries. Zofi provides practical, workable recommendations that cut through the complexity and make a difference right away. She gives the reader a set of quick, realistic, and sensible solutions to make the hours spent working in virtual teams more productive and more enjoyable.

—**Chris Lubrano,** International HR, MetLife

"A comprehensive and well-written book that provides practical insights into one of the most important topics in the modern virtual business environment."

—**Dr. Amos Baranes, Ph.D., CPA,** CEO Learning by Simulation;
Associate Professor, Sapir College, Jerusalem

"The LEARN acronym for improving daily interactions is outstanding! The cross-cultural communication technique is extremely helpful when addressing the challenges of managing a virtual team. Overall, the commonsense approach that Ms. Zofi applies seems very simplistic yet extremely effective when not only addressing how to handle the virtual environment but also how to handle individual work styles."

—Kent E. Blackmon, PMP, SSBB, Manager,
Business Process Improvement, Coca-Cola Refreshments

"As a consultant operating in a highly global and virtual work environment, Zofi's use of tactical examples, best practices, and insights make *A Manager's Guide to Virtual Teams* an invaluable resource for enabling more effective virtual teaming. Through analysis of several case studies, Zofi also ties together the many complex facets of virtual teams—including cross-cultural, technological, and relationship building—making the book very relatable and one which will resonate with anyone who has seen the challenges of working in or managing a virtual team."

—Whitney Cook, Human Capital Management Consultant,
Deloitte Consulting

"Living in Hawaii and working for a mainland company with primarily East Coast customers, and family for that matter, I consider most of my communication to fit within the realm of virtual team communications. That said, I have always considered communication with virtual teams one of my strengths. Reading this book reminded me of the importance of the communication strategies I use today and gave me insight into new tools and strategies to keep my team healthy, happy, and productive. I just want everyone I interact with, personally and professionally, to read this book too!"

—Jack Germany, Team Lead,
Interface Services, Healthcare Information Systems

"If you are a virtual team member, leader, or otherwise, this book is a fast-track learning experience on how to do it right the first time. Enriched with pertinent examples . . . it's a must-read book. I have it several times over."

—Hussain Tawawalla, Founding Partner and Director,
Development, Enterprise for Business & Development
Management (EBDM), Peshawar, Pakistan

"Often, many of the virtual teams that I have coached at AMEX, Nielsen, and Covidien have learned through trial and error what worked and what didn't. *A Manager's Guide to Virtual Teams* is an invaluable resource in improving all aspects of the virtual team environment. Especially insightful are the suggestions on building accountability and trust. In fast-paced business environments, having a comprehensive resource to help teams become aware of how their own accountability will contribute to an environment of mutual trust is essential."

—Holly O'Grady, Holly O'Grady Consulting,
Learning Strategies & Talent Development

A Manager's Guide to
Virtual Teams

Yael Zofi

American Management Association

New York • Atlanta • Brussels • Chicago • Mexico City • San Francisco
Shanghai • Tokyo • Toronto • Washington, D.C.

This publication is designed to provide accurate and authoritative information in regard to the subject matter covered. It is sold with the understanding that the publisher is not engaged in rendering legal, accounting, or other professional service. If legal advice or other expert assistance is required, the services of a competent professional person should be sought.

Library of Congress Cataloging-in-Publication Data

Zofi, Yael S. (Yael Sara)
  A manager's guide to virtual teams / Yael Zofi. — 1st ed.
      p.   cm.
    Includes index.
    ISBN-13: 978-0-8144-1659-4
    ISBN-10: 0-8144-1659-4
    1. Virtual work teams—Management.   2. Communication and culture.
  3. Organizational change.   I. Title.

  HD66.Z63   2011
  658.4'022—dc23

                                                           2011019829

About AMA

American Management Association (www.amanet.org) is a world leader in talent development, advancing the skills of individuals to drive business success. Our mission is to support the goals of individuals and organizations through a complete range of products and services, including classroom and virtual seminars, webcasts, webinars, podcasts, conferences, corporate and government solutions, business books, and research. AMA's approach to improving performance combines experiential learning—learning through doing—with opportunities for ongoing professional growth at every step of one's career journey.

Printing number
10 9 8 7 6 5 4 3 2 1

Contents

To my baby boy, who will forever remain virtual,
and to my baby girl, Ella, who has become a reality.

Acknowledgments

Connection! That's what it's all about.

All my life I've been a student of people—how they collaborate and develop lasting relationships. My work has revolved around facilitating connections to build strong teams, and for many years these sessions occurred in face-to-face environments. With technology and globalization transforming the workplace, physical presence is not always possible, which brings up an interesting question. In virtual situations, how can you strengthen the human connection? Physical presence by itself is one factor in a relationship, but *feeling connected* is the key factor. I began to wonder how to sustain connection despite time and space constraints, and set out to explore virtual teams.

This book was written as a practical, non-theoretical guide to manage virtual teams. However, it is deeply rooted in management theory and over 20 years of observation and practice in the field. I was fortunate that experienced authors, such as Geoff Bellman, Bob Lee, Deb Himsel, and Shoya Zichy gave me helpful writing advice. I learned from practitioners, Dick Beckhard, Warner Burke, Tom Barbieri, and from great colleagues at Accenture, Price Waterhouse Coopers, and JP Morgan.

The greatest thank you goes to Susan Meltzer for being my true friend, confidant and writing partner. You truly deserve a medal for staying by my side throughout the entire experience. I couldn't have written this book without your guidance, editing comments, and reality checks. Your pointed remarks, late night jokes, and practical suggestions encouraged me to stay focused on the end goal.

In writing this book I have been supported by my great AIM Strategies® team. Jenna Thornton managed the AIM operation and kept me on track to meet my deadlines. A dedicated group of interns, consultants and peers helped in the research, data crunching and analysis, and coordination of many details. A heartfelt thanks to: Emily Linder; Galit Ronen; Michiko Sato; Tenzin Gonsar; Ken Reid, Yuko Takahashi, Raphael Binet; Pooja Jhaveri; Kira Lewis; Perin Colah; and Catherine Montcastle, and Simranjit Mallhim, among others.

Also, the editing team at AMACOM who believed in this book from the beginning and have helped shape the manuscript. Thanks to Editors: Christina Parisi, Barry Richardson, Karen Brogno and particular thanks to Jim Bessent who oversaw the manuscript through the production process.

Many people gave their time, their expertise and their suggestions. The utmost thanks go to the 150+ virtual managers, dispersed team members and global leaders who contributed. I also want to thank clients who gave me access to their world to gain a close up perspective on the topics that follow in these pages. Their experiences come alive through the cases, stories and learnings that are so vital to this book.

Lastly, the most important acknowledgement goes to the people closest to me, my family. I am lucky to have a supportive family who helped me juggle so many responsibilities during this project—running a consulting practice, teaching a graduate course at night and most importantly having my second daughter. Truly overwhelming at times! Thank you to my husband Ted who kept our family going and stood by me every day, supporting me during my many sleepless nights writing, writing, writing. My mother, Tamara, for watching over my girls. Most of all, my daughters Maya and Ella challenge me to be better each day and teach me that the upcoming "Keyboard" generation is catching onto things fast.

—Yael Sara Zofi

An Overview of Virtual Teams

W alk into any office today and you know that things are not as they were a decade ago. If you engage employees in conversation, many of them will say that they are working on some projects with colleagues who do not work in the same building, the same city, or even the same country. Ask them if they have met these teammates and some employees may claim to have viewed pictures posted on the Internet, while others may describe introductions made during webcam meetings or a visit to a corporate off-site event.

Clearly our business landscape has changed.

The virtual team, VT for short, is a work arrangement in which a group of people share responsibility for goals that must be accomplished in the total, or near total, absence of face-to-face contact. With the rise of technology and globalization, virtual teams are now reshaping the way we think and do business.

Organizations have always operated in multiple locations, but now, colleagues are increasingly asked to work together across geographic boundaries, with shared responsibility for outcomes. Global operations have emerged throughout the world of commerce, running 24/7 on different continents and across times zones. Many large conglomerates place teams in different countries with the expectation that schedules will fit the project—and follow the sun—as one team hands off work product to another. This arrangement is possible because technology brings efficiencies in creating work product and solving complex business issues quickly.

Although many virtual work arrangements exist today for employees at all levels, the number and diversity of these types of arrangements (whether home offices or office locations) just keep increasing. Enabled by technology, the virtual team is a natural solution for getting deliverables out the door in our fast-paced, global environment. Increasingly, leaders are charged with quickly putting together teams of individuals with appropriate skills and abilities to fit within a project's time line, regardless of where the talent is physically located. In such situations, e-mail has usurped voice mail while conference calls have replaced conference rooms.

The Need for Virtual Teams

Virtual team arrangements have become increasingly popular as companies rethink their human capital resources and real estate expenditures. Of course, teamwork has long been a common work value, with many companies using teams organized around successive tasks; so, the virtual team is only the latest accommodation to the realities that govern work process. The virtual team is unique, however, because the most appropriate expertise is pulled together from many locations and even organizations—and yet team members may never meet in person. With virtual work arrangements, recruiting talent and expertise is possible, regardless of where people are based.

More than any other factor, information technology has enabled the proliferation of virtual teams. With mobile devices, text messaging, e-learning modules, and cloud computing, team members are able to interact in more accessible ways, anywhere, anytime. Thanks to high-speed networking technology and wireless connectivity, instantaneous communication across the world is possible, at low cost, at a touch of a button, screen, or keyboard. Today, we take for granted this phenomenon; not too long ago, it was the province of futurists. This faster-paced environment, combined with a slowed economy, brutal cost cutting, and relentless outsourcing, has forced companies to rethink every aspect of their operations.

As businesses expand globally to new markets, they launch operations where labor is cheap and the cost of living is lower; opportunities are provided for local employees to collaborate on a wider scale and develop expertise. Reverberations are felt beyond their shores as relentless pressure builds for quickly producing more goods that are less costly, forcing creative solutions for quicker breakthroughs. Virtual teams, then, are beneficiaries of technology-based, cost-conscious, and globally sourced business operations (see Figure I-1).

Figure I-1. Benefits of virtual teams.

Technology Enablers

- Online communication capabilities and technologies are continually improving virtual team operations. Among the key enabling technologies are mobile devices, text messaging, instant messaging, cloud computing and software as a service (SaaS), file and application sharing, electronic bulletin/message boards, group decision support systems, real-time calendar/scheduling systems, and e-mail.
- Online learning, distance learning, and e-learning software enable learning anywhere, anytime.
- Virtual business networking (LinkedIn) and social networking sites (Facebook) and video/web conferencing further increase online communication.
- Technology memory recording tools track every step of complex processes; keeping records (documentation) and learning from past processes enables speed (doing things faster) and memory (preserving shared experience).
- Document management systems enable online libraries for information sharing, thus saving space and time.

Cost Considerations

- Cutting down on personnel, office space (real estate), infrastructure, furniture, and supplies that are no longer needed saves money.
- In high-rent cities, businesses can rent shared office space on an as-needed basis with all amenities, including reception, support staff, technology, and telecom services.
- Virtual teams eliminate the need for having dedicated conference meeting space and on-site training facilities, and related travel and accommodations costs.
- Environmental benefits include reduced commuter gas consumption and a smaller carbon footprint. Think green!

People Expertise

- Global workforce means talent is anywhere and everywhere—and the workforce is mobile.
- Expertise is available and can be outsourced for numerous functions (web design, blog development, search engine optimization [SEO], advertising, technical media/financial writing, technical market research, administrative, public relations, marketing, and sales support).

The Virtual Landscape

Another force fueling the emergence of virtual teams is the need to move resources quickly. Competitive factors are a compelling motivator to find alternative work arrangements so that work processes and procedures can mirror the accelerated rate at which the world now operates.

Organizations are aware that the marketplace is increasingly multi-cultural and diverse. They know their business colleagues and customers may come from many different cultures with an inherently different worldview. Trade is dynamic and reflects the easy flow of goods and services across our globe. Hand in hand with business interests creating new global trade links is the relatively new practice of offshoring, where core and noncore business functions are outsourced far from head-quarters to take advantage of low labor costs and the availability of highly educated workers, with technology serving as the great equalizer.

Greater diversity in the workforce is a by-product of virtual teams, since professionals with different backgrounds, styles, and languages "work at the same table." Leaders of virtual teams are challenged to cre-ate a smooth operation in spite of the many differences at play. Given that possibilities for misunderstanding and cultural blunders are magnified in such situations, those charged with ensuring business success would do well to expand their own tools and techniques to deal with diverse teams.

Leaders and managers must be flexible and able to adapt to this di-verse workforce and global consumers. Leaders must understand differ-ences in worldviews, communication styles, ethics, and etiquette of the people they deal with, both internally and externally. They must under-stand the historical, political, and economic reference points of different people. And they have to do all that while managing their own tasks and responsibilities.

Even if you are a virtual manager at a small company, you are prob-ably interacting virtually with global audiences. The good news is that you are not alone. The bad news is that you are faced with challenges of virtual management. And that means you need to excel at multitasking in this ever-changing virtual world.

If you are responsible for a virtual team, you are responsible for the team's results. Before you even begin, here are a few of the challenges of virtual leadership:

➤ *Relationships.* How will you get to know your virtual team members? How will you build rapport? How will you develop small talk about their personal interests?

➤ *Performance.* How will you assess what kind of job they are doing? How will you evaluate their leadership skills, their development, and their results? When and how will you actually observe their performance?

➤ *Communication.* How will you keep your direct reports updated? So much happens in a day; how will you have time to keep all team members in the loop?

➤ *Delegation.* When your team members work off-site somewhere and you don't even have a chance to see them or observe their daily work activities, how will you know who is capable of doing what? How will you delegate assignments and track their deadlines?

➤ *Team Building.* Virtual team members are dispersed. How can you build a strong team when your people have never even met each other?

➤ *E-Mail.* You get hundreds of e-mails a week. How will you use e-mail effectively to manage your staff?

➤ *Conflict.* With people so dispersed, how will you even know when you have a conflict with a direct report? Or when your direct reports have a conflict with each other?

➤ *Promotion.* How do you evaluate when someone is ready for promotion? Conversely, how do you keep from being "snowed" by someone who's trying to get ahead? How do you know when it's time to eliminate a poor performer?

➤ *Teleconferencing.* When will you have time for longer teleconferences? (You hate teleconferences.)

➤ *Walking the Talk.* In the old days, we did management by walking around. We showed people what we wanted by our own actions and body language. How will your direct reports observe you and your management style? How can you "model" if you don't see people?

> ➤ *Travel.* How often are you going to have to fly around the country to meet your direct reports? If your team is spread across the globe, how much international travel will be required?

In this new business environment, the old skills of yesterday are no longer sufficient. They worked fine when business was simpler. They probably even helped you get promoted to this level. Remember when you could actually walk down the halls and "drop in" on your direct reports? You could observe how they ran meetings, watch them interact with subordinates, even sit in on difficult conversations. When completing performance evaluations, you could list examples of things you personally observed. You could look into their offices, see family photos or awards, and be prompted to ask about the kids or favorite hobbies. They also dropped by your office or had lunch together to build a relationship.

Management was hard even then, but it's a lot more complicated now. Welcome to your virtual reality; welcome to virtual teams!

Defining Virtual Teams

Virtual teams have many names and definitions. I interviewed more than 150 virtual team managers and members in preparation for this book, and no two interviewees defined *virtual teams* the same way. Virtual teams are referred to, variously, as geographically dispersed teams, global teams, internationally distributed teams, temporary cross-functional teams, dispersed project teams, knowledge worker teams, communication technology teams, technology-mediated teams, computer-supported or computer-mediated teams, offshore teams, interdependent groups across time and space, cyber network teams, and the list goes on.

Hand in hand with the concept of virtual teams is their powerful enabler: information technology. I mean the popular collaborative tools that most individuals refer to when describing how their virtual teams work. Without these communication tools (e.g., e-mail, instant messaging, teleconference bridges, message boards, web conferencing, webcams) virtual teams would remain a novelty in the world of work. Yet, make no mistake. Despite the fact that technology is the lifeline of the virtual team, its essence still focuses on people and places.

Here are some of the more interesting definitions and descriptors of virtual teams, gathered from the interviews I conducted with VT managers and members from different industries:

> "People who need to work together who aren't currently in the same office. They can also be working in different departments, or different cities and countries, and still operate virtually as well."
> —VT MANAGER, HUMANITARIAN RELIEF ORGANIZATION

> "Any team that doesn't have a set office that people show up in regularly. There are really two sides to it: 1) pulling together an ad hoc team and creating a virtual team to work on a project on an 'as needed' basis, and 2) virtual teams working across time zones using technology."
> —VT MEMBER, TECHNOLOGY COMMUNICATIONS COMPANY

> "A group of people who get together without a solid line reporting relationship to solve a problem. The key attribute is that virtual teams have some accountability to deliver results, but their players do not have a formal reporting relationship to the team leader."
> —VT LEADER, ELECTRONICS/BIOCHEMICAL COMPANY

> "I see the virtual team having two definitions: 1) There are people who work only from home. They are telecommuting and never go to the office. 2) There are people who are geographically dispersed. They go to an office somewhere else and may never meet. Virtual teams work according to what needs to be done and once the project is completed, these teams are gone."
> —SCIENTIST, TELECOM COMPANY

My Definition of Virtual Teams

I have always opted for a simple definition of the term *virtual team*, as follows:

> A virtual team—whether across the street or across the world—is a team whose members simultaneously work together to a common purpose, while physically apart.

The traditional definition of a team applies here: There is a common goal or purpose; team members have complementary skills and share interdependent performance goals for which they hold themselves mutually accountable. The difference is virtual: *simultaneously working together, while physically apart.*

A virtual team does not always mean that individuals work from home. Many virtual teams consist of employees who work both at home and in small groups at the office, but in different geographic locations and organizational boundaries. Even when teams are situated locally, many people refer to the "fifty-foot rule" and the probability of communication between coworkers dropping with the distance between them. After about fifty feet (fifteen meters), it doesn't matter whether team members are on different floors of the same building or in different states. Your teammate in the office across the street may be just as virtual as the coworker in India.

Working in Virtual Teams

Virtual teams bring possibilities of recruiting talent and using resources irrespective of where they physically reside, and in the process breakthroughs are achieved faster and costs are lowered. Virtual teams do, however, come with their own pros and cons, or opportunities and challenges.

One of the more profound issues is how to get team members to bond and develop the collective energy so vital to pushing projects forward and achieving results. A great exercise that I often use with newly formed virtual teams involves asking them to review a list of opportunities and challenges (see Figure I-2) and check off the three or four most important ones. I then combine input from all team members and begin a discussion about the opportunities people are most excited about and the challenges that are their greatest concerns. This exercise can be done in person or by conference call (video or telephone) to allow team members to chart, describe, and discuss issues as a group, creating a bonding experience. It also gives the virtual manager additional information to incorporate into the team operating principles, or *Rules of the Road*, and help virtual teams establish ongoing mechanisms to overcome these challenges.

Figure I-2. *Opportunities and challenges of virtual teams.*

OPPORTUNITIES	CHALLENGES
Technology enables quick information gathering and an increased knowledge base (access to data and experience of others).	Technological challenges are involved with setting things up (investment in equipment, support, and training) as well as the learning curve.
Speed is essential since virtual teams are expected to form quickly, select the right members, understand each member's role/tasks, develop appropriate processes, and carry out work efficiently.	Speed brings potential misunderstandings, particularly in the early stages of Team Setup (role and task clarity, getting deliverables out the door).
More ideas can be generated because members are not stifled by dominant members, as usually happens in face-to-face teams.	The brainstorming aspect becomes more difficult when members are physically separated.
Communication technologies can equalize the opportunity for participation of every member.	Running regularly scheduled remote meetings takes tact, cultural sensitivity, and creativity.
Virtual teams provide flexibility in balancing personal and professional life.	Virtual work occurs anywhere, anytime, and might interfere with personal life.
Virtual teams offer self-direction and a high degree of autonomy.	Virtual teamwork might be missing; social isolation creates a feeling of "I'm by myself."
Virtual teams can change members more easily, depending on the task or expertise needed, and thus tap into a greater talent pool.	Leaders/managers may find it more difficult to motivate employees and establish team spirit.
Virtual teams get involved in project work and share accountability with team members quickly, making better quality decisions.	Building trust may be challenging because it requires mechanisms different from those used in face-to-face teams.

(continued)

Figure I-2. (continued)

Communication is often in writing, which makes documentation easy.	There is a greater risk of misinterpretation and conflict in communication resulting from the lack of verbal and visual cues that you would get during an in-person exchange.
Team membership can be flexible and can shift in response to changing project needs.	Team members may feel less connection to the organization because of rapid change and social isolation.
The various people who compose a virtual team provide diversity of expertise.	The diversity of people who compose a virtual team may bring in different cultural norms, which must be addressed.

How Virtual Teams Differ

Virtual teams use many different communications tools as their primary sources of information exchange. These tools can be organized as same time/same place, same time/different place, same place/different time, or different time/different place.

COMMUNICATION OPTIONS	EXAMPLES
Same Time (Synchronous), Same Place (On-site)	Face-to-face meetings
Same Time (Synchronous), Different Place (Virtual)	Audio/videoconferencing, chat rooms, camera phones
Different Time (Asynchronous), Same Place (On-site)	Electronic bulletin boards, shared files on a network
Different Time (Asynchronous), Different Place (Virtual)	Internet, web, voice mail, e-mail, snail mail, fax

Virtual teams can be assembled for a variety of purposes as well, as shown in the following list.

TYPES	DESCRIPTION
Networked Teams	Membership is fluid. These teams are frequently used in consulting firms and technology organizations to answer questions by utilizing external or internal contacts.
Parallel Teams	Membership is distinct. The team's work, in the short term, is to look at organizational processes and problems and make recommendations. Team members have other responsibilities, so they frequently communicate while working on their main job.
Project/Product Development Teams	Membership is also distinct, but the team works over a long period of time. Tasks are clearly defined, and results are "specific and measurable." These teams are authorized to make decisions, not just recommendations.
Production Teams	Usually found in one department or function (such as accounting or human resources), these teams perform ongoing work and frequently telecommute, but have clearly defined membership.
Service Teams	They "follow the sun." One group works to fix problems, and when the workday ends, another group in a different time zone continues the work. They are particularly effective as service/technical support teams.
Management Teams	Team members are managers belonging to the same company found in different cities or countries. They work collaboratively and communicate frequently.
Action Teams	These teams mobilize quickly to offer an immediate response in reaction to events (e.g., news or weather teams) or emergency situations.
Offshore Teams	They are commonly used for software development and outsourcing. The company subcontracts portions of the work to an offshore service provider who can work collaboratively with the onshore team.

In addition to the different types of communications options and the different types of virtual teams, these arrangements also bring with them people from various organizations and departments whose cultures may differ in terms of how communication is handled, trust is built, conflicts are resolved, and work gets done. These cultures span organizational and national boundaries and are an added layer that is often overlooked. I dedicate a whole chapter to cross-cultural communications in virtual teams later in this book and provide you with guidelines and suggestions for handling geographically distributed cultures across time and space.

Success Factors of Virtual Teams

The factors that ultimately determine a virtual team's effectiveness would seem similar to those that govern on-site teams: Clarify team goals, roles, individual responsibilities, and deadlines. Communicate frequently. Build trust among members. Agree upon ground rules for meetings and other interactions (e.g., "We will answer e-mails within twenty-four hours," or "Ming and Jane want calls to come to their office phones, but Ida prefers us to call her cell"). But there are unique and particular issues that come up in virtual teams that are critical to their success.

One rule above all guides virtual team behavior. It is especially vital when members haven't met in the flesh and when they cannot see each other's facial expressions, read body language, or otherwise pick up the nonverbal signals inherent in face-to-face communication. The rule is: Assume positive intent of your teammates. It means simply giving others the benefit of the doubt.

I asked the various virtual team managers interviewed for this book this important question: "What is the secret of your virtual success?" Here are their main points, along with some observations of my own that come from my consulting experience:

> ➤ Assemble your virtual team for an initial face-to-face meeting (if possible) and make sure you interact with your team at least once a year in person.

> ➤ Create structure and establish standards to manage the team remotely and ensure that everyone is clear on the roles/ responsibilities, approaches, and main elements: who, what, when, where, how, and why.

➤ Focus on the vision and mission of the team at the beginning of each meeting.

➤ Break down team goals into smaller (short-term) objectives.

➤ Employ technology that supports state-of-the-art reliable communication and collaboration, and train team members how to use it.

➤ Develop a way for team members to get to know one another (e.g., post bios and pictures on a team website and/or incorporate them into presentations).

➤ Pay attention to silent members on your calls; know who contributes, who doesn't, who stays involved, and who stays in the background.

➤ Create inclusive discussions while also encouraging open and free (especially free of politically correct dialogue) communication.

➤ Summarize team meetings, action items, deliverables, and decisions; distribute information to all team members, and have a backup communication plan/system in place for when members can't attend.

➤ Develop mechanisms for building accountability and trust on the team.

➤ Handle conflicts and misunderstandings outside the main conference call. Follow up with individuals afterward, but do it in private. Make sure you are respecting their cultures.

➤ Get deliverables out the door efficiently while meeting quality standards and time guidelines.

➤ Give frequent praise for accomplishments and celebrate team success.

These and other best practices, suggestions, tips, and techniques to help you to successfully manage your virtual teams are further discussed throughout the book.

CHAPTER 1

The Three Stages of Virtual Team Development

W hen quicker, smarter, and more flexible work groups are in demand, virtual teams are the answer. These highly adaptive work communities are able to extract appropriate resources from the organization and are well suited to twenty-first-century business operations driven by globalization and technology innovation.

In this first chapter, I'd like to introduce an approach to virtual team development that I use with clients. It sets the tone for the rest of the book since all the other chapters follow this approach. As virtual team arrangements become increasingly popular, leaders continue to grapple with a profound issue—how to get team members to bond and form the energy so vital to pushing projects forward. With this in mind, I created this Virtual Roadmap as a practical blueprint to guide team members in achieving results in a complex and unpredictable business environment.

To gain a broad understanding of the nature of virtual teams, consider that the life cycle of a virtual team is divided into three separate stages, each with its own set of characteristics. They are:

> ➤ Stage 1: Setup
> ➤ Stage 2: Follow-Through
> ➤ Stage 3: Refresh

To bring these three stages to life, let's think of setting up a virtual team as taking a trip in your car along the virtual superhighway. How do you plan any trip? You need to clarify your destination, map your route, and follow the Rules of the Road. If it's a new car, you might conduct a test-drive, but very quickly you'll be speeding down the open lanes of the highway toward your destination. As you drive, you are alert to the other drivers on the road, so you avoid sharp turns and accidents. You may have to get off the road for a time or navigate around roadblocks before continuing on. Along the journey, you might have to stop to tune up or perform maintenance on the car. And if your destination is far enough away, a refuel is required. Once you reach your destination, you slow down and park your vehicle safely. But your journey has just begun!

Stage 1—Setup: The Importance of Planning for Virtual Teams

Driving the virtual highway can be a daunting journey if you do not prepare yourself and your team for what lies ahead. Although it is impossible to foresee every difficulty that may arise, good planning is essential to set the stage so that your fellow passengers can concentrate on necessary activities and avoid hazards. Setup begins with determining and sharing the team's purpose, since every virtual team is formed around a business purpose. Without a shared purpose, virtual team members could easily focus on local tasks and concerns while excluding joint efforts to achieve organizational objectives. Teams that work across boundaries turn the intangible thing we call "purpose" into doable actions. "Purpose" is actually a system of five interrelated ideas that build one upon the other: vision, mission, goals, tasks, and results.

Just as poor first impressions are hard to overcome, early missteps in setting up your virtual teams may lead to unintended (and undesired) consequences, such as distrust among members and poor communications that adversely affect getting deliverables out the door. Clearly, a key responsibility of the virtual leader is to properly set the stage for a newly formed virtual team.

Before virtual teams embark on their virtual journey, you (as the leader) must navigate through three key steps: (1) clarifying the team's destination, (2) setting the Rules of the Road, and (3) conducting a test-drive.

Clarify the Team's Destination

Just as you would make the final destination of your journey known to a group of passengers traveling in your car, you need to share the project's goals with the entire virtual team before giving specific assignments or roles. Virtual teams carry an extra layer of complexity, of course, because team members are not sharing regular, in-person contact with one another. As a virtual leader, you must, above all, remain sensitive to the difficulty of developing a context of shared understanding. The leader is charged with making team introductions, and then defining and clarifying team goals, and most important, achieving a shared understanding of who is expected to do what to accomplish these goals.

For those situations in which you have the authority to select the team members, you will also be tasked with screening and hiring people. Once they are in place, you have to determine how each member will contribute to the "journey" and assign specific roles that are linked to the priorities outlined in the destination phase. Since a single manager can't possibly oversee all activities even at close range, additional self-management becomes essential for virtual teams.

Set the Rules of the Road

Leaders of virtual teams must create appropriate norms so that disparate elements, from a variety of functions, can coordinate efforts and create deliverables. Every team has a set of rules (or norms), even if they are unspoken. This code enables a diverse population to work with reasonable assurance that critical safeguards are in place to ensure mutual understanding about the nuts-and-bolts processes that are necessary to create products and services. Imagine that you are defining specifications for a new part and require answers from locations A and B, where interlocking elements are manufactured, before you can proceed. If providing input at a critical impasse is not a high priority for them to address quickly, your deadlines will not be met. Understandably, having clearly stated norms that allow team members to hold each other accountable is a "must-have" for virtual teams.

Once these basics are completed, the team must find its own way to become a cohesive unit and achieve these stated goals. Opportunities that traditional (on-site) teams have for face-to-face contact (at the water cooler, in the hallway, in the cafeteria) do not exist in the virtual world, so it is harder for members to establish common ground and develop a common identity. Without these opportunities, you need to find other ways to build team unity.

To counter a lack of comfort that we may have with other people of diverse backgrounds, cultures, and skills, it helps to create norms. Norms become central to the team's workflow. They are a virtual team's Rules of the Road, helping to guide team members' interactions around, for example, (1) communications, (2) deadlines, (3) decision making, (4) conflict management, and (5) information sharing. The rules need not be complex; in fact, simple rules simply stated work best, because they avoid the potential for misunderstanding caused by differences in cultures and languages. Each of these five interactions needs to be codified so that team members are free to focus on their responsibilities for team success.

Setting these "rules" includes developing a Team Code, or a common language of specific phrases and acronyms used to standardize processes and procedures.

Conduct a Test-Drive

The last step in Team Setup (see Figure 1-1) is the virtual team's test-drive. This is the group of activities that a manager takes to assess team members' capabilities and their ease (or lack of ease) with team communication. During this step, you engage in group and individual conversations with team members to gain a better understanding of each person's personal and professional needs, wants, goals, and motives.

Figure 1-1. Team Setup.

Stage 1: Team Setup	Activities
• **Team's Destination**	• Clarify team's destination (goals, roles, responsibilities).
• **Rules of the Road**	• Establish Rules of the Road (norms, communication, expectations, goals, time lines, decision-making and information-sharing processes, priorities). • Allocate resources (equipment, tools, technology).
• **Test-Drive**	• Run a test-drive (1:1 meetings, team building).

Stage 2—Follow-Through: The Importance of Implementation and Performance

Follow-Through is how you ensure that the team adheres to norms created and agreed upon during the Setup phase. Leaders must remain vigilant so that the team practices agreed-upon procedures; they must be sure that straightforward feedback mechanisms exist to offset the lack of physical proximity and that communication flows in both directions. Holding members accountable requires effective Follow-Through in a number of areas, including performance management cycles, conflict resolution techniques, and bridging cultural differences, so that momentum is maintained and business objectives are met.

Stage 2 along the Virtual Roadmap is the heart of virtual team performance because it reveals how virtual teams execute or drive toward goals. As summarized in Figure 1-2 and discussed here, there are four key aspects of Follow-Through that are at the core of the virtual manager's responsibilities: (1) opening communication lanes, (2) driving accountability, (3) avoiding sharp turns, and (4) performing maintenance.

Open the Lanes of Communication

Because of the difficulties of creating strong communication in virtual work arrangements, it is essential to put in place structures and processes that facilitate communication. Virtual managers should establish a culture of frequent updates. It may be necessary to repeatedly remind the team to keep lines of communication open in unusual situations, such as during exceptionally hectic workdays, systems failures, or family emergencies. A quick telephone call clears up potential misunderstandings and also alleviates feelings of frustrations when an urgent question is not answered. It may be necessary to divulge details, if time permits, which would be unnecessary if coworkers sat in close proximity.

Information technology is the main contact vehicle for virtual team communications, but it brings with it a variety of issues, from technical difficulties to unfamiliarity with use. To prevent feelings of frustration, managers need to make comprehensive training available. In addition, virtual teams should agree on a point of contact to streamline the problem-solving process.

Drive Accountability (and Trust)

In the virtual environment, actions speak louder than words, and the cohesion that is so critical for teamwork develops when people can count on each other. Commitment leads to trust. Plainly said, if a team member promises to do or explain something, that person should deliver on that promise.

What is the best way for leaders to engender this commitment? By embedding predictable checkpoints in team procedures and processes. In an on-site team, trust grows through frequent face-to-face interactions where members learn what kinds of etiquette and responses are expected. Although virtual teams lack regular face-to-face exchanges, they nonetheless have expectations to meet. If, for example, the team agrees that e-mails should be responded to within twenty-four hours or that team members should notify each other when planning long absences away from their workstations, then these commitments should be the norm.

Another common obstacle faced by virtual teams is a lack of accountability. When daily physical contact is not possible, members often overlook the fact that colleagues located elsewhere are dependent on them for information and service. A leader can "check in" and remind less responsive participants about jointly agreed upon norms. Additionally, the leader can establish a timeline and reprioritize deliverables to meet deadlines. Such supervision also helps to alleviate feelings of suspicion about a team member's contribution (or lack thereof) to a project.

Avoid Sharp Turns (Managing Conflict)

Even when teammates act in ways that engender trust and engage in effective communication, it is not realistic to believe that all conflict can be avoided along a virtual team's journey. Just as drivers need to stay alert to avoid hazards on the road, the challenge for virtual teams is to spot these disagreements or "sharp turns" before they grow out of hand. The virtual manager must learn to pick up on missing signals and take remedial action, rather than assume an issue will eventually work itself out without an intervention. Taking even simple steps can save the team from missing deadlines or producing poor-quality output. The sharp turns that a virtual team must avoid happen in three areas, which will be explained more fully in future chapters:

> ➤ *Performance Conflicts.* Such conflicts occur around the issues of "how" tasks are accomplished and "who" should do them.

> ➤ *Identity Crisis.* This type of conflict arises when virtual team members also work on other teams.

> ➤ *Data Overload.* Welcome to the wonderful world of ubiquitous technology!

On every journey, roadblocks appear; however, being aware of potential issues before they rise up makes you better prepared to resolve them.

Perform Maintenance (Deliverables)

The primary purpose of any team is to contribute to the process of getting deliverables out the door. For virtual environments to produce these deliverables within financial, quality, and time constraints, certain conditions must exist. Goals must be clearly stated and understood by all. Procedures and processes should be put in place that take into consideration multiple time zones, language barriers, cultural differences, and various skill sets and degrees of fluency with the primary language (a tall order indeed!). And virtual managers must infuse the team with the spirit to sustain the human connection, which leads to strong relationships so critical to coordinated efforts. Regardless how competent the team is at project management (a key requirement in day-to-day work tasks), there is no better foundation for getting deliverables out the door than a well-thought-out operational structure to facilitate that human connection.

Figure 1-2. Follow-Through.

STAGE 2: Follow-Through	Activities
Open Lanes of Communication	Create strong communication (develop a context of shared understanding, hold regular meetings, share information).
Drive Accountability (and Trust)	Engender commitment, trust, and accountability (update, modify goals, keep team on target).
Avoid Sharp Turns (Manage Conflict)	Resolve conflicts and misunderstandings (handle roadblocks, evaluate problems, build or strengthen relationships).
Perform Maintenance	Sustain team performance (update deliverables, modify goals).

Stage 3—Refresh: The Importance of Realignment

During a team's natural life span, changes occur because the project's original goals may undergo revision; in addition, new members join and others depart. You need to keep members connected while shifting gears by performing tune-ups and refueling. Business imperatives often require teams to apply a steady energy and focus to work through their alignment issues, and managers must use appropriate tools and techniques to ensure that a long-standing team renews this dedication. In addition, membership is not static. Virtual teams are flexible work arrangements, with members continually arriving or leaving the group, and so their makeup tends to frequently change. When team members contribute their expertise and move on, it is necessary to handle transitions smoothly.

Stage 3 of development along the Virtual Roadmap includes the following steps: (1) doing a tune-up, (2) refueling, and (3) putting it in PARK.

Do a Tune-Up

Even stable virtual teams require the leader to periodically check in to make sure that members have weathered the bumps in the road. These tune-ups allow possible conflicts to surface early so that they do not fester and potentially derail the project. It's also helpful to evaluate the technology in use on a regular basis to identify new ways to facilitate communication.

It is possible that some team members do not perform at an adequate level, which may signal that it is time to "replace parts" by either reassigning roles to other capable team members or bringing new members on board. A thorough review of expectations should take place, not only to clarify the tasks but to ensure that the additional responsibilities are doable. If a new member joins the team, then the onboarding process needs to take place.

Identifying areas for improvement, making new role assignments, and acquiring new members may further signal the need for additional training to keep knowledge and skills current. Training should build upon prior learning from the group's experience, incorporating best practices and insights on better ways to accomplish goals. In addition, if new tools and techniques have been created since the team's inception, then all members should be trained in those areas appropriate for their own responsibilities. At this point, the team should reestablish norms or create new ones that reflect the team's growth.

Refuel

The more time spent on the team, the greater the possibility of dips in a team member's energy and commitment level. Virtual team leaders must be sensitive to people's need to recharge their batteries, but within limits and in ways that are suitable to the organizational culture.

For example, team members can engage in *happy hour*, virtual style. Although gathering after work for dinner or drinks is not possible, VT members can agree on a specific time to instant-message (IM) each other for informal chats of a nonbusiness nature. At first, questions can be scripted; then, as participants' comfort level increases, these formal interactions should give way to natural conversation. Often, one or more members are congenial and enjoy bringing a social dimension to the group. Virtual leaders should stay alert to this possibility and encourage those who seek to energize colleagues.

Often, VTs are made up of people who work on a combination of virtual teams and on-site teams. In these situations, the leader is the key link for her or his own virtual team. It is the leader's responsibility to step in and interact with other managers to ensure that multiple priorities do not prevent the team's work from moving forward. One multinational organization, for example, requires leaders, acting on behalf of their own virtual teams, to negotiate time and work issues with the home office or other virtual team leaders. By communicating with peers to discuss common issues, virtual team leaders can ensure that their own team members are able to devote an appropriate amount of time to each project.

Put It in PARK (Wrap Up)

Many times virtual teams disband when a project is completed. At this point it is helpful for the leader, the team members, and the organization to formally debrief the team's work experience. Documenting team results, accomplishments, and lessons learned is a public way to acknowledge individual efforts and record best practices for future assignments.

As a final step in the Refresh stage (see Figure 1-3), it is useful to ask team members what they would change if given a chance to redo the experience. This has a twofold purpose: It can help people formulate ideas

Figure 1-3. Refresh.

STAGE 3: Refresh	Activities
• **Tune Up**	• Tune up (set new goals, onboard new members, reestablish norms, realign, replace parts).
• **Refuel**	• Refuel (reenergize, respond, regroup, redo; determine improvement areas; assign training and provide new role assignments).
• **Put It in PARK**	• Put it in PARK/wrap up (prepare final reports, review accomplishments, arrange closing celebrations and evaluations, restart).

for a future virtual team experience, and their insights can help you improve your own skills as a virtual team leader.

If time permits, you can privately communicate with team members and thereby individualize your comments as appropriate. However, this process is not a substitute for a more formal close. This "celebration" ideally includes the opportunity to bid good-bye to coworkers whose paths may not intersect again, as well as a chance to evaluate the team as more than the sum of its parts.

One idea for the wrap-up is to give awards. Serious awards are great, but humorous ones are fine, too, as the objective is to bring the entire team together and enjoy each other's company (physical or virtual) for the last time. Members can end their shared experience on a positive note, and the door is left open for communication if members work together in the future.

In my consulting experience, this three-stage approach has been shown to be practical, doable, and easy to implement. The rest of this book is organized to follow the three stages of VT development, with the end result being a true journey. Chapter 2 further addresses the details of planning and then Setup of your virtual team. Chapters 3 through 6 detail the Follow-Through steps critical to team implementation and performance. Chapter 8 is dedicated to Refresh stage activities and what you need to do to realign your team for the future. In between, in Chapter 7, I introduce ideas for handling cross-cultural communications, which is an extra layer of complexity to virtual team development.

What's Next for Your Virtual Team?

Organizations set up teams like yours to create, develop, and deliver complex results within various constraints. Virtual team arrangements are already becoming more popular, and in time they will become the norm and reshape the world of business. As members of one or more virtual groups, we will form, build, and rebuild webs of relationships in ways we cannot yet imagine.

Virtual teams are the wave of the future, especially as technology advances and enables closer human connections. The next few decades may mirror science fiction movies. Perhaps team members may one day communicate through holograms or, who knows, the transporters familiar to *Star Trek* fans may become a reality.

Today, however, you may be like many virtual managers, with a team that has been working together for a long period of time and largely functions on automatic pilot. Some of these managers may hope that results will improve on their own (as if producing the same actions produces miracles), while others may struggle to incorporate the increasing demands of our precarious world into already-strained professional relationships.

Add to this scenario the reality that your team may continue to expand into new regions, adding additional challenges to developing teamwork. Almost every organization with a virtual presence needs to design newer team structures to link knowledge pools across broad geographic and organizational boundaries. And, as the leader, your responsibility is to help your team make the necessary transition to the unique demands of virtual teams.

True virtual teamwork requires a deeper level of clarification, communication, commitment, and consequences management than is typically present in teams sharing a location. Teamwork must also become more than a notion; teamwork must require the *team* to *work*.

My hope is that the ideas presented in this book will be useful to virtual teams whose members are distributed across various time zones. But the ideas will not work if they simply stay in this book. You and your team must bring them to life and, in doing so, create productive, energizing, and fulfilling workdays.

The power of your leadership lies in your hands, as you determine how you will put into practice those ideas, strategies, and suggestions that can meet the needs of your organization. With that in mind, get ready to move away from the sidelines of team management and into the game of global virtual leadership—where the power is in creating team*work*.

CHAPTER 2

Setting Up Your Virtual Team

Virtual teams are teams that "work together apart," whose members may be scattered across the street, across the continent, or across the globe. Although members do not share the same location, they must still work collaboratively to meet common objectives, managing their roles and daily responsibilities in challenging circumstances. What keeps these individuals organized, communicative, and productive without the ongoing face-to-face connection that people who work in close proximity share? The answer is twofold: (1) Tools, guidelines, and processes are set up to enable connection, and (2) the manager acts as the main "connector," keeping members who are beyond arm's reach aligned to each other—in essence, bringing "together" people who are "apart."

A human connection in a virtual world is the most important one of all. This connection is made possible through collaborative applications and new modes of 24/7 communication. Despite distance and time considerations, the potential for a broad, deep, and wide connection exists inside as well as outside your team: Businesses connect to customers, prospects, vendors, partners, and others. People connect with web tools. You connect with your brand. Your virtual team connects with other virtual teams. The message is this: Just *connect!*

Why has connection become so important to organizations? Over the last 100 years, strategic leadership initiatives have transitioned from focusing on development to transformation and, finally, to connection. During this period, leadership was about managing change, and the leader was the Agent of Change. Today, the role of the leader is one of linking resources and talent, the building blocks of business success, to achieve goals. In a virtual setting, an added dimension to achieving tangible goals is the logistical challenge of connecting people, who may never have met, across various locations. I call this concept the Agent of Connection. For more than a decade I've been advocating that our roles as leaders and managers have transitioned from managing change to creating and enabling this human connection in the virtual workplace.

How do you foster relationships with people you rarely see? This is probably your greatest challenge as a manager because it sets the tone for how your virtual team will operate, communicate, coordinate, and conduct business.

Importance of Setting Up Your Team

This entire chapter is devoted to setting up a team. My experience as a consultant to virtual teams has taught me that top talent, good intentions, and high expectations don't guarantee success in the virtual space if this crucial step is missed. My clients often put great effort into selecting the most talented virtual team leaders and members, and providing technology to facilitate connectivity. They then expect high performance to materialize in due course. Where is the training or team development time that enables leaders and members to come up with an operational "roadmap," set up norms, and establish expectations? Without these solid preparations it is all too easy to fail. I often get the "call of desperation" from managers looking to engage my services after their virtual team has been up and running for several months, because that's when the team starts experiencing communication, trust, and conflict issues.

How do you create that connection among people who come from disparate cultures, have different communication styles, and can't eyeball each other to establish a strong face-to-face connection? Your role as a virtual manager begins with taking that first step of setting up the team.

Putting the Wrong Foot Forward . . .

Here are some typical complaints and concerns I often hear from VT members and leaders about what is missing from their teams. Do these situations sound familiar?

> "We don't have a way of working together as a team because we are missing a sense of purpose that can drive us toward working cohesively."
>
> —VT MEMBER, MOBILE DEVICE MANUFACTURER

> "I don't know what my role is now that two members just moved out and it is all a moving target. Now motivation is decreasing and people are tired because they have not been on the same page from the start."
>
> —VT MEMBER, WIRELESS TELEPHONE COMPANY

> "Our team was never set up [right]. We just reorganized several team members, so the work and emotional elements are tense and people want to figure out how to address that. Everyone has different expectations, and if everyone can voice concerns and managers address them, it might help clear the air."
>
> —GLOBAL TEAM MEMBER BASED IN INDIA, HIGH-TECH SERVICE PROVIDER

These comments are typical of many others I have heard, and they sound a cautionary note of what *not* to do. Now let's see how you can start out on the right foot.

Putting the Right Foot Forward . . .

Think of setting up your team as if you were preparing for a long road trip. You'll need to have a roadmap to guide you. To create this Virtual Roadmap, which I first introduced in Chapter 1, you need to:

1. Determine your team's purpose, mission, and goals (otherwise known as your Team Destination).

2. Articulate an overriding structure for how the team will operate (what I call the Rules of the Road).

3. Develop a Team Code of Conduct.

4. Be prepared to realign your Team Setup, if necessary.

The Team Setup Report

When working with clients on planning a Team Setup session, I often use a proprietary tool that I designed to analyze each member's strengths and areas in need of development, with an eye toward team participation. Before meeting in person, the entire team answers survey questions that deal with the kinds of issues that affect team performance: communication, trust, conflict, cultural differences, motivation, and project deliverables. Many of the questions explored in this tool are woven into the sections of this chapter, and you can find a sample report on my website: www.aim-strategies.com.

Team Destination

"Would you tell me, please, which way I ought to go from here?"
"That depends a good deal on where you want to get to," said the Cat.
"I don't much care where," said Alice.
"Then it doesn't matter which way you go," said the Cat.
"So long as I get somewhere," Alice added in explanation.—from *Alice's Adventures in Wonderland*

Just as Alice in Wonderland wasn't sure what her true destination was, if you are not clear about your goals, you will never be sure when you get to the right "somewhere." The destination is very important, and the secret to getting there lies in the planning. You can deploy competent people, tools, and processes as an effective leader, but always start with the destination in mind and then plan backward. With various tools you can measure activities and track deliverables along the way.

Clarify Your Team Destination

To get started, ask yourself the series of questions outlined here:

What Are You Charged with Accomplishing?

➤ Develop products or services for a new market.

➤ Work on a new business process or system.

➤ Work with people across the organization to solve a problem or find more efficient ways of producing something.

➤ Organize an event involving various groups.

➤ Share experiences around key topics such as best practices, medical research, or business trends.

➤ Take the group in a new direction.

Who Are the Sponsors, Stakeholders, and Interested Parties?

➤ Who has a shared interest in making sure my virtual team is successful?

➤ Is our sponsor strategically positioned in the organization?

➤ How do we make sure there is strong support for our results?

➤ Will our sponsor be available to promote the team's activities, find resources, remove barriers, and provide advice?

What Will Success Look Like?

➤ What is the "burning platform" that we, as a team, need to work on most?

➤ What are the team's purpose, mission, and goals?

➤ What planning is necessary to create synergy?

➤ What deadline are we working toward?

➤ What resources are available for this journey?

➤ As a leader, do I have the tools to make decisions?

Who Should Be Part of My Team?

➤ Who are the best available people for my team?

➤ What are the special requirements of working virtually?

➤ Whom do I need to talk to before I bring team members on board?

➤ What are good questions to ask when setting up the appropriate team?

Identify Purpose, Mission, and Goals

Newly set up or transitioning teams are charged with goals and expectations that should be clear to members as well as to your senior management. Some virtual teams are formed out of great necessity—to meet a deadline or fill a gap in production capacity, for example—and the vision is an afterthought at best. This haphazard organization can lead to misunderstandings and hold the team back from succeeding. (To address that situation, see the material, later in this chapter, on developing a Team Charter.)

My recommendation is to recruit the team you need to attain defined goals. Of course, if the team makeup is determined by management, then you need to quickly acquaint yourself with your team. In either situation, though, you must ask yourself, and others, what objectives the team or project must meet. Do we have what it takes to get the team to buy into those objectives, and what actions must be taken to do it? For example, if I determine that the team can do quality control (QC) on a certain part for a new gadget in X days, others may not share my optimism and therefore will be reluctant to agree to this goal because the odds of completing the QC process in that time frame are low. However, if I can convince the team that the new type of metal used in the manufacturing process improves resilience and tests well, then I will have a greater chance of convincing others to buy into my vision.

As a virtual manager, you are responsible for motivating the team and keeping the shared vision in the team's sight. You might ask for feedback on the stated goal(s) so that everyone can buy in and gain greater clarity of the vision, even if team members have no say in initial goal setting. This is particularly important with virtual teams because people can disengage or fly under the radar. So, whether in person or through a video/phone conference or other means, bring the team together and help members feel as if they are stakeholders, with something to gain or lose.

Having in place certain key elements leads to results: You need a clear project plan, the discipline to fulfill that plan, a clear division of responsibilities, across-the-board accountability, and continual internal checks. You want to set yourself and your team up for success from the beginning, so destination is paramount. Knowing that what was initially promised was delivered in the end, with feedback and approval throughout, is the main key to success.

Determine Project Sponsors and Generate Support

How do you ensure that your team has what it takes to achieve results? As the leader you need to keep things on track, vigilantly monitoring the actions of team members. Many times virtual teams are hastily formed when a senior executive says, "Let's get a team going to resolve problem X." The team starts out with a clear mandate, but if a strong sponsor doesn't continue to champion the team's work, people have a hard time buying into the mission. Members can be pushed into joining the team, but that alone will not engage them into fulfilling its mission, either. Ideally the team has a powerful sponsor who vocally and consistently supports its goals and is able to elicit members' energy, skills, and efforts along the way.

Sponsors are champions who can link the team to a management power structure across locations and organizational boundaries. They can help virtual team leaders break through barriers to resolve issues, obtain necessary resources, and relate the team's work to the rest of the business. Some sponsors are strategically positioned within the organization and therefore do not follow the day-to-day activities of the team. Others may be lower in the hierarchy and work more closely with team leaders and the teams in their chain of command. As you run into roadblocks, your sponsor can help resolve them. However, my consulting experience has shown me that virtual team leaders who continually turn to a powerful sponsor to smooth over difficulties will diminish their own power. Accountability is a joint responsibility.

Consider Who Will Come Along for the Ride

In an ideal world you could pick the best people for your team from the labor pool. In reality, however, you usually have to go with available talent. Also, you may inherit a team or arrive during a transition when the team is ready for realignment after gaining or losing team members.

Even though your choices may be limited, you may still have a say in who joins the team. Therefore, if possible, talk with potential team members about their expertise. Your main goal in recruiting is to balance a range of experience, knowledge, and skills, including softer skills, such as ease of communication and ability to work well across cultures. Whether you have the option of picking the people for your team, your biggest test as a manager is how well you blend people of different skills, experiences, and cultures into an effective unit.

Qualities to Look for When Selecting Virtual Team Members

There are mixed opinions as to whether it is better if a team member is an introvert who prefers to work alone or an extrovert who is more vocal. Most managers I've interviewed prefer team members who enjoy initiating input and who seek to communicate and reach out to others, which is why I like to list an extroverted personality as a desirable quality to look for. With that in mind, here are the qualities you want in your team members:

➤ Self-starter

➤ Adaptable and resilient in the face of change

➤ Comfortable with autonomy

➤ Able to deliver on time

➤ Can work on technical issues and complex problems

➤ Gets satisfaction from being involved with team projects

➤ Has the interpersonal skills to build relationships with others

➤ Able to open up to strangers and share knowledge and ideas easily

➤ Good self-management and time management skills, as well as the internal drive to stay on target

➤ Extrovert

Team Charter: Setting the Course for How You Will Operate

Developing your Team Charter may be the most important activity in the team destination phase. The charter summarizes direction and purpose. I highly recommend getting the team together in person early in its life cycle (if possible) to develop this charter and set the course for how the team will operate. That way you reduce the number of issues that might arise later due to conflicts, misunderstandings, trust breakdowns, shifting priorities, and the loss of resources. If the project is complicated, a face-to-face session is especially recommended, although restricted travel budgets may make this option unrealistic. Under these circumstances, use alternative means to conduct a meeting via videoconference, a conference call, or audio with text and graphics. If the Team Charter has been predetermined, as is sometimes the case, the team then needs to focus on getting buy-in and putting the charter into operation.

Here are the building blocks of creating a Team Charter:

> ➤ Identify a clear vision and have the team agree on its mission and goals.

> ➤ Have goals and plans written out clearly for each team member.

> ➤ Create an operational project plan to support the team's purpose.

> ➤ Clarify the standard operating principles of the team.

> ➤ Let teammates know their roles and responsibilities.

> ➤ Identify resources (what you have, what you need, what you will get).

> ➤ Discuss how to identify milestones to acknowledge progress along the way.

> ➤ Agree to check in periodically and align the Team Charter as direction changes.

> ➤ Outline any channels of support (organizational, technological).

> ➤ Clarify sponsorship.

Team Rules of the Road

Establishing the Rules of the Road for how you and your team plan on driving along the virtual highway is an important part of the setup process because all team members need to work within the same guidelines or things fall off track. Just as on a road trip you can drive along a highway or use local roads, team members need to create rules that apply across the team while being mindful that certain guidelines may be unique to specific locations.

During this phase, team members decide on ground rules for how they will operate and how they will hold each other accountable for various work processes. They create procedures to meet deadlines and quality standards. Guidelines related to which communication modes to use in various situations are discussed as well (e.g., phone calls for emergencies; e-mails to communicate information; instant messaging to respond instantaneously). Sharing these guidelines saves time and eliminates a guessing game that is all too common in the virtual environment. Be clear when designing team processes because misunderstandings can occur quite easily. Consider appropriate procedures for projects with tight deadlines as well as for those where there are fewer time and budget constraints.

Conduct a Team Orientation Session

I recommend having a nonvirtual (face-to-face) kickoff or initial team orientation session. Even if members don't meet again after the Team Setup process, teams that meet in person at least once are better off in the long run. The purpose of this orientation session is to learn about each other's work preferences, establish norms for communication, and explore ways team members will make decisions and hold other team members accountable. Some welcoming activities that are fun and boost the team spirit are highly encouraged, especially since they jump-start the initial bond that can grow into a stronger web of team relationships later on.

Virtual teams can be set up within a large organization or a smaller outfit, such as a technology, consulting, or service provider firm. In all cases, though, they can benefit from an initial meeting in which members meet face-to-face to set the tone and launch appropriate procedures. Here are a few ways that various companies, large and small, encourage face-to-face time when building a virtual team:

> "It is most important to meet in person, set expectations, and establish ownership. Once you do that, there is credibility with people that helps make the virtual team successful."
>
> —MEMBER, LITIGATION CONSULTING FIRM

> "I found that when the team comes together for a kickoff, it helps to build credibility and trust. We brought the whole team together for one day. The rest of the time members worked in smaller groups and traveled to meet with clients. [But, because of that initial meeting], we have a better connection when people go back to their home locations. We know what people look like, and we can continue to develop strong ties to our members."
>
> —MANAGER, PROFESSIONAL SPORTS LEAGUE

> "My entire practice is based on forming SWAT teams of senior-level freelancers. I never work alone. I coordinate virtual teams, like on the original *Mission Impossible* shows, and pick out [the people] I need based on skills, languages, knowledge, and abilities. I make sure that I interview and know the key players, who they worked for previously, and conduct reference checks. We hardly meet in person since everyone is spread out, but those of us who are local get together once a month, for happy hour, to connect."
>
> —OWNER, PUBLIC RELATIONS FIRM

CASE STUDY

Leading a Virtual Team Orientation and Creating Rules of the Road

One client, a director at an optical imaging company, contacted me when she was charged with upgrading several product models simultaneously. Let's call her Tamara. With little ramp-up time and a limited travel budget, she needed to create one cohesive team to meet tight deadlines within cost constraints. Here is Tamara's situation and what she did to set up a high-functioning team.

Situation

Members of three different virtual teams were brought together to work on Tamara's project. Each team was located on a different continent—Asia, Europe, and North America—with each team reporting to an on-site boss. When Tamara assumed leadership of this project, team members were brought in based on specific functional expertise and experience with complex assignments. Tamara needed these teams to work closely with each other to ensure a seamless research and development process; engage with a web of global suppliers and distributors; and handle many issues related to marketing and sales, manufacturing, QC, strategy, and general operations.

Team Destination Process

We created a plan where Tamara first held a conference call with each location and then followed up with a conference call with the entire team (all three regions). It was a logistical challenge to set up calls with the team operating across many time zones and required making decisions about who would wake up at 4:00 a.m. and who would stay awake until midnight. Calls were set up in advance with a promise to rotate them in the future so that no one region would bear the brunt of a punishing schedule. During initial calls Tamara communicated, clearly and simply, 1) the mission—which was to upgrade several models by X date, 2) how it impacted the bottom line (the business needs to introduce new models to stay competitive), and 3) why it was time-sensitive (the top two competitors had already made inroads in the market with offerings).

Tamara understood that each member needed to feel important to this project. As she explained, "I made them feel special. They all looked at the same spreadsheet showing each member's job, and deadlines for major deliverables, with plenty of room left for individual comments." Since she was stationed in North America, she added that "I told everyone I planned to visit the other two sites within three months and that I would spend time with senior management at each location to give everyone some visibility."

Tamara then set up meetings with directors and vice presidents to talk about the new models. She patiently created opportunities to build relationships with potential sponsors across the organization. As a result, many decision makers outside her area learned about the team's efforts and innovative solutions to complex problems. "I knew that in our company we played 'musical chairs' with assignments," she said. "Any one member could end up on another team; it was just a matter of when. Keeping open relations helps everyone in the long run, because when you know someone's reputation, it's like shorthand when you finally have to work directly with that person."

Team Charter

Tamara held brief phone conversations with every team member before planning a face-to-face session. From information gathered she created a "straw dog" document that included the Team Charter, operating principles and procedures, and a deliverables time line. To build consensus, this document was shared with every team member before the in-person meetings. Tamara didn't use a majority-rules approach to get members to sign off, because some folks had issues with certain areas and she was determined to reach a resolution that satisfied everyone. She made it clear that everyone would succeed or fail together, and her actions convinced teammates that the purpose was worth participating in. Tamara told me, "We were successful because team members believed in the vision and wanted to follow it."

Team Rules of the Road

Tamara and the team planned a three-day on-site meeting to establish team norms and operating guidelines and to lay out agreed-upon major deadlines. Over this three-day period, many subgroup meetings took place. For example, engineers from Singapore, the United States, and Germany worked together to figure out how they would communicate going forward, and procurement specialists set up QC standards and narrowed down an approved supplier list. Other subgroups explored the Team Charter that Tamara created from her phone meetings. Because of the size of this group, teams were divided into three groups that explored various aspects of their Rules of the Road. Participants in each group shared their thoughts and added/edited/changed rules, as necessary, to create consistency and consensus. Each group presented its findings at an all-hands meeting before the teams returned to their respective locations.

During this meeting, the team explored questions related to its information needs, organizational alignment, and roles and responsibilities, as follows:

Team Information

- What is this team's purpose or mission and goals (reiterated)?
- What is the time frame for meeting these goals?
- Where can the team go for the information it needs?
- What resources are available to the team?

Organizational Alignment

- What strategic goals of the organization does this team support?
- What are the expectations around what this team needs to accomplish?
- How is the team going to make decisions?
- How is team success measured?

Roles, Responsibilities, and Expectations

- What are the different roles and responsibilities on this team?
- What do you expect from your teammates?
- What can your teammates expect from you?
- Is there a gap in expectations and reality?
- What can you do to enhance team effectiveness?

Team Operating Principles

The guidelines and agreements that came out of their meeting are as follows:

- We agree to follow the Team Charter and believe it represents what we are about. It will be honored, and revisited if alignment is needed.
- We agree to disagree respectfully and resolve problems (early) as they occur.
- We will call each other when things are not what they should be; in this way, we set up permission to be honest with each other.
- We are engaged and committed to the project. If anyone feels disengaged at any time, raise the issue and let's talk it through.
- We will be conscious about the version of English used (British English, American English, or Indian English).
- We will share language around team norms.
- We will create a shared "e-room" for documents to be accessed, as needed, by all stakeholders.

- We will rotate time zones and availability on evenings and weekends for necessary calls/updates.
- We agree to communicate regularly according to this protocol: weekly meetings via WebEx to update each other on progress and key deadlines; daily meetings with subteams on their related work; phone call for emergencies—otherwise use e-mail but expect a response within twenty-four hours; instant-message and text for a quick one-line response.
- If budget permits, team members will meet annually at a rotating location. At the very least, department heads from each location will meet for an annual update.

As Tamara told me, "By the time we left the meeting, everyone felt exhausted but exhilarated. Every major deadline, operational procedure, and potential catastrophe was looked at and how we would address it. It wasn't easy to find a common way to look at the various components of updating our models, but we had to do this, and everyone knew it, and we found a way for everyone to make decisions. Everyone had input, and we also made sure to include some bonding time as well. I asked people to bring a picture of themselves, with or without their family, or an action shot doing a favorite activity. Someone actually brought a picture of himself holding a bowling trophy. By the end of the three days, everyone felt they were a part of the team. We knew what we had to do and, as much as possible, we came up with very concrete ways to make sure that we could count on each other to do what was necessary."

Not every virtual manager deals with a situation as complex as Tamara's, but anyone who bears responsibility for deliverables in the virtual environment can take cues from her situation and plan ways to make the team work effectively.

CASE STUDY

Setting Up a Virtual Team . . . Virtually!

For many virtual teams, it is not always possible to conduct face-to-face meetings. In such cases, I recommend having a videoconference or finding some mechanism so that people can interact "virtually in person" to develop shared guidelines, norms, and operating principles. Of course, scheduling and coordinating specific issues and ensuring appropriate technology across all locations requires additional planning.

Jerome, an aerospace conglomerate manager, was given the difficult task of setting up a virtual team during a merger. His core team consisted of thirteen direct reports; half of them were based across the United States, while the rest were located in regional offices in Singapore, Germany, Mexico, and the United Kingdom. These individuals managed an additional pool of 150 virtual members who were widely dispersed throughout fifty countries. Not one of Jerome's direct reports worked out of the same time zone, and, to further complicate matters, no budget existed to hold a face-to-face team kickoff to establish the cohesion.

Jerome consulted with me to plan how to set up his team under such challenging circumstances. We determined that it was essential to ask his direct reports to share their thoughts about the merger in several open-ended conversations. Phase two would involve conversations with the greater team. He scheduled three phone calls with each individual, listening to their concerns, hopes, and suggestions. Jerome told me, "I listened until I was tired. I did not hang up on any call because I wanted all my direct reports to feel heard. It took me over two weeks to complete all thirty-nine calls. Then, after I digested everything they had to say, I planned a phone conference with all fourteen of us. We had a series of discussions."

Jerome discovered that the merger had generated many intense feelings. Direct reports were very protective of both their own culture and the local company culture. "There were many emotions about the merger," he said. "Some people took a back seat while others were very vocal about how they felt. I had to draw some people out. It took a lot longer than a face-to-face experience, but after three weeks of intense conversations, we started to move faster; we started to become a team."

During this three-week period the core team created a Team Charter and Rules of the Road and addressed any issue that was brought to the table by the local teams. "At each phone call, I fed my team the questions that guided the process, and that was the framework for our Rules of the Road," Jerome explained. "I made sure that all my direct reports pushed these questions down to their own teams. We used trial and error to draw people out because I didn't know at first what would work with each direct report, and they also didn't know how their people would react. We used some video-conferencing, especially with Asia, because I wanted to establish a real connection with people I had less familiarity with."

This virtual team was successfully set up without any face-to-face contact among the members. "I still haven't met some of the people on the local teams," Jerome told me, "but I travel to Singapore, Mexico, Germany, and the U.K. every year, so I finally met all of my direct reports, but since they don't travel, they've never met each other."

Here was a virtual manager with energy, empathy, and common sense. He was charged with setting up a rather large team that handled complex projects across many locations, cultures, and time zones. By organizing his thoughts, planning carefully, and exhibiting an optimistic attitude, he accomplished what he set out to do. "I've never had an experience like that one since," Jerome told me. When asked what the toughest part of this situation was, he didn't hesitate before responding, "We had so many people involved; too many time zones; things became really complicated because there was so much coordination necessary. But even though things took longer, we got the job done, and we met the objectives the head office gave us during the merger."

If you are the leader of a dispersed team that will rarely or never have the chance to meet in person, you must be the connector and find a way to travel to your team members' work locations periodically. Your whole team may not be able to meet, but at least team members will feel personally connected to their leader.

Steps for Existing Virtual Teams

What if your team already exists? Teams are dynamic entities, and new members often join or depart from them. How an existing team handles this transition differs from a newly formed team.

Managers of existing teams may choose to undertake some of the activities described in this chapter. Many of these activities are also appropriate when "Refreshing" the team, redirecting the work, and addressing problems. When a team's makeup changes and it is necessary to indoctrinate new team members, then revisiting these elements becomes essential. In addition, managers can conduct a lessons-learned session to explore ways to improve the team's process after an intensive project is completed or once a key product/process is delivered. The session presents a good opportunity to reestablish team operating principles, Rules of the Road, and communication plans. If face-to-face gatherings are possible, you can use such gatherings to review team effectiveness and reorient current and new team members as needed.

The following is a list of activities to consider when orienting new members to an existing virtual team:

Prepare the New Team Member. Set up either a face-to-face or telephone meeting with the new team member to cover these items:

> ➤ Provide an overview of the team's vision, mission, purpose, and charter (a team destination document).

> ➤ Discuss team goals, schedules, and current deliverables.

> ➤ Review team members' roles and responsibilities.

> ➤ Confirm each new team member's role, deliverables, expectations, and accountabilities.

> ➤ Discuss current plans, status meetings, and updates.

> ➤ Provide access protocols for telephone, e-mail, video setup, etc.

> ➤ Outline what characteristics are important for the team member to demonstrate to be successful.

> ➤ Provide an overview of team norms and codes. Give new team members a one-page overview of the team's process, code, and approach. (A common practice is to design this document and maintain it on a shared drive to help integrate new members faster.)

> ➤ Review technology requirements and any software setup issues.

> ➤ Review how the team member will get introduced during the first meeting.

Get Your Team Ready. Preparing the current team for the new team member is equally important. Introduce new team members to other members either via an initial team call or more informally. Also:

> ➤ Involve current team members in the onboarding process. Allow them to get to know each other before the newest member joins the team.

> ➤ Make the first day special.

> ➤ On the first day, start the new team member at an office where other team members work, if possible. This helps new recruits make connections that will grow into valuable relationships.

Pair Up for Success. Assign new team members a "buddy" to help orient them to the organizational culture. Provide information about team operating principles, project history, organizational policies, any specific Team Codes involving use of meetings and audio/video-conference calls, and where to go for answers to questions about specific issues.

> ➤ Introduce new team members to their respective buddies and make sure to clarify that this is their "go to" person while they are learning about the ins and outs of your organization.

> ➤ Review and answer any questions relating to preparing the team member for success.

> ➤ Discuss the organizational history surrounding the project, team, and business environment.

Integrating new team members is a constant reality for most virtual team projects, and teams that have organized and established techniques are more successful at helping new members ramp up faster and integrate more smoothly. Your role as a manager is to orchestrate this transition and make it as transparent as possible for everyone. A good idea is to have an integration plan that maps out the first six weeks of new team members' employment, including who they will meet, aspects of the business they will be exposed to, and how they will report back to you. You'll want to include daily check-ins with new team members during the first week and at least weekly check-ins the following weeks.

Taking steps to lay the groundwork for a successful team member integration and onboarding will pay off for you in the long run.

Develop Team Spirit

One project manager in a technology firm told me, "I don't think it's necessary to see people in person to get work done, but socially it's a nice thing to have. The main problem is that the physical distance, combined with lack of face-to-face [contact], can become lonely." I detected some wistfulness in his tone, and a preference for some nonvirtual interaction. Later in our conversation he confessed that he would like to sit down for a cup of coffee with someone, go to lunch with colleagues, or stop by their desk for a brief chat. Even though he enjoyed working virtually, he missed team spirit.

As you establish your team's Rules of the Road and agree on team norms and operating principles, make sure to generate excitement and create conditions that motivate team members. Engaging in fun activities is a way to generate a common bond, but maintaining this bond in the virtual world takes some work. The trick is to uncover commonalities among members.

Find Common Threads

My Team Setup tool includes an exercise to facilitate team cohesion: the Team Common Threads Finder. It should be completed by all team members. As the team leader, you have several choices as to how to use this exercise: 1) Send the questionnaire to your team members and tabulate the answers before the first meeting. 2) Ask the questions at the first meeting. 3) Explore these questions one-on-one during several calls. or 4) Share these questions during a conference call with all participants.

Sharing common interests is one way to facilitate team cohesion. Figure 2-1 lists popular topics that are sometimes discussed at informal meetings; use this list to find potential similarities (or common threads) among your team members. The answers will give you an idea of the team's interests—and what members may have in common. Think of it as a first impression without an actual face-to-face meeting!

Here are the instructions team members are to follow: For each category, please choose the item that represents your top preference. Although several topics may interest you within each category, for the purposes of this questionnaire, choose your favorite. You may add comments after each question.

Figure 2-1. Common Threads Finder for establishing rapport among team members.

TV Shows	Movies	Music	Ideal Vacation
• Comedy	• Comedy	• Classical	• Ocean
• Fantasy	• Fantasy	• Rock	• Camping
• Love Story	• Action/Adventure	• Country	• Family Visits
• Drama	• Animation	• Pop	• Exotic Places
• Sports	• Drama	• National	• Urban Areas
• Reality TV	• Romance	• Hip-Hop	• Adventure
• News/Politics	• Thriller/Horror	• Jazz	• Cruise
• Other	• Other	• Other	• Other
Which shows do you like?	Name your favorite movie of all time.	What's your favorite genre?	What is the most interesting vacation spot you've visited?

Books	Free Time	Additional Hobbies
• Biography	• Hiking	• Drawing/Sculpture
• History	• Sports	• Photography and Design
• Fiction	• Reading	• Writing/Blogging
• Love Story	• Computer Games	• Animal Care
• Novels	• Social Networks	• Song and Music Writing
• Poetry	• Meeting Friends	• Cooking
• Business	• TV	• Gardening/Nature
• Other	• Other	• Other
Name the most recent book you've read.	What's your favorite way to spend your free time?	What are some additional hobbies?

My clients have shared with me how successful this exercise is in establishing helpful rapport between team members. Think how much easier it is to establish a bond with your coworker in Moscow when you can discuss a mystery brilliantly solved by Adrian Monk or laugh at Seinfeld's adventures with his friends.

Real-Life Examples of Team Spirit

There are many ways to build and maintain team spirit among virtual team members. Many virtual teams have found creative alternatives to create visibility within the team and to build a sense of community and commitment.

Welcome Aboard! One consulting team I worked with had a "welcome party" for new members when they joined during various times of the team's life cycle. Team members would pass around their profiles/bios in advance, which included answers to key questions about personal interests and hobbies. One creative colleague put together a book of photos of each member's family that was distributed in person at the annual meeting.

Happy Birthday to Us! On another virtual team, one colleague with a customer service background used birthdays to foster connection. Her colleagues referred to her as their rah-rah birthday person. Whenever someone had a birthday, she sent every team member the same gift (e.g., chocolates or funny pens), with the birthday celebrant getting the same type of gift, only bigger. A note accompanied the packages to all stating, "Please save it for the next conference call on [date]." Then, during the call, team members opened their gifts at the same time. This team found a way to maintain the bond that began during its initial phase, and even new members quickly caught hold of the team spirit.

Zulu Warriors. A client of mine who led a virtual team for a financial services organization shared her story: "I launched a global sales competition between regions to keep everyone excited and willing to come up with sales goals. It was about signing up customers and getting people to use the service. Everyone got involved and goals were approved by senior management. I managed the process and made sure [goals] were clear to all. Sales increased and I had reports compiled and distributed. Team calls became about how the teams could do even better, and where each one stood on best practices. This was an exciting part of the rollout—it wasn't something I planned in advance, but it added excitement and competition. I did region-specific awards and worked with each region's management to decide on the awards. One region did a cash prize, another got smartphones. Teams picked names [like Zulu Warriors] and had to explain why they picked them. One winning region also won for 'best performance country team.' I went to Madrid to present the awards at a regional meeting. It was a great feeling for me and it energized the team even more."

Common Snack Food. One interviewee, a virtual manager at a telecom company, shared a story that has become one of my favorite team spirit tales. This was an idea conceived to build morale, get everyone on board quickly, and break down cultural barriers. Traveling to each calling center for meetings was not possible, so the manager asked all four centers (England, the United States, Asia, and Russia) to share a simple food with the others. On a rotating basis, the team whose turn it was would send the other three locations a box of snack food common to its culture. "We introduced a simple food to share [during the] monthly virtual status meeting," the manager said. "It became something [local teams] thought about and gave attention to. Whatever they chose was sent in a box to everyone else. They planned ahead and sent nice notes to each other. Each site included additional people [in developer roles] who participated. I called it 'The Common Snack Team-Building Exercise.' New York shipped bagels and pretzels, England sent tea and biscuits, Asia sent bento baskets, and Russia provided tea and latkes. It took a while, but we found a way to build the team while creating meaningful work and succeeding together. Everyone enjoyed it, and it built team spirit."

Team Code of Conduct

The Team Code of Conduct is about how the team communicates. Team members decide, for example, on how they will conduct phone calls, handle e-mail, and deal with a variety of issues that naturally arise in the average workday. There is a code for acceptable and unacceptable behaviors that guide every aspect of team life. Virtual teams may require more detailed Team Codes than on-site teams because they specify behaviors about the intangibles inherent in virtual situations that are less important when you can walk over to someone's desk. Examples include when to use e-mail, phone, texting, certain team shorthands, and/or three-letter acronyms (TLAs).

Issues the Team Code Should Explore

➤ How often will we communicate?

➤ What issues require what kind of communication?

➤ Who will be notified? When? How?

➤ When is it appropriate to escalate issues?

➤ When should we use telephone, video, audio, and other technology tools?

➤ What is the etiquette and protocol for participation? When someone is on speakerphone, when should the mute button be used to give people from other cultures additional time to gather their thoughts?

➤ How does the team keep everyone informed? Who takes and distributes minutes, and do roles rotate?

➤ When will the agenda be distributed (X hours or days prior to the meeting)?

➤ Who will record meeting minutes (or action items or agreements)? Where will they be posted (on the team website or distributed another way)? When will they be posted (hours/days after the meeting)?

➤ Which meetings are mandatory and which ones are not? Can a certain number or percentage of team members attend, or are meetings rescheduled if there will be absences?

➤ How does the team handle different time zones?

➤ What are acceptable time frames for online communications, returning e-mails and telephone calls, and rescheduling?

➤ What are the guidelines for using (or not using) e-mail? What are the guidelines for structuring messages (e.g., what kind of messages to flag and what to write in the subject line)?

➤ What is the appropriate time to respond to requests?

➤ What technology may be used by team members to stay connected?

➤ How do we handle time lags and delays of asynchronous messages that constrain communication and might make it difficult to form group consensus or reach conclusions?

➤ What procedures exist for scheduling meetings using group-scheduling software?

➤ How do we handle trust breakdowns and communication gaps and stay focused?

➤ How will the work be reviewed? Who reviews the work? Who approves the work?

➤ How do we hold each other accountable for using our Team Code guidelines so that communication is reinforced and our communication mechanisms/methods don't break down?

These questions should be explored (ideally) during the in-person Team Setup meetings, and then the answers need to be posted publicly for current and future team members to understand operating norms. You can decide how you want to publicize these details and hold people accountable. Some teams choose to communicate more informally while others create a Team Code of Conduct that they post on their shared drive or shared workspace and refer to it when needed. We will examine in more depth actual Team Code samples and suggestions in Chapter 3, "Context Communication."

Realignment: Make Adjustments as Necessary

If you have adequately addressed the issues noted in this chapter to set up your team, you have an excellent chance of leading a high-performing virtual team. However, Team Setup is not an exact science, and it is possible that you may need to rethink certain rules that were established when you began the process. Just as you would take a new car out for a test-drive, your team may try out certain procedures and determine that certain adjustments are required. You might have to realign work schedules in different locations and adjust how often colleagues communicate with each other.

Here is where the real work sets in, when the team works on a daily basis within the parameters that you (and your team members) have worked so diligently to set up.

In a Nutshell: Mastering the Four Elements of Successful Virtual Teams

My consulting work over the years with various global and local teams has shown me that four themes recur in organizations that have high-performing virtual teams, regardless of sizes and types. If your teams are to be successful, these four elements must be continually mastered throughout the team's life cycle. The next four chapters deal in depth with these four elements or themes, as briefly introduced here (with the relevant chapter in parentheses):

1. Ensuring effective communication (Chapter 3)

2. Creating accountability/trust (Chapter 4)

3. Managing conflict and handling misunderstandings (Chapter 5)

4. Developing work systems to get deliverables out the door (Chapter 6)

Often, virtual managers like you work tirelessly to engage members and drive business results without sufficiently addressing these core elements during the Team Setup phase. Frustration can set in when the team functions less than optimally and you question what's not working. Many managers fail to take the time up front to deal with these four critical elements. However, their importance can't be overemphasized. If you don't address them early, you may end up dealing with them later, when energy and time will be spent fixing problems and addressing performance issues that have festered and grown in severity.

YOUR VIRTUAL ROADMAP TO TEAM SETUP

Best practices for establishing contact with members before the team's initial meeting:

1. Call or visit each team member personally.
2. Provide some mechanism by which team members can find out about one another.
3. Facilitate interaction in a nonthreatening way.
4. Send all team members information about the team, including its charter.
5. Make certain that a forum exists for answering team members' questions.
6. Find out whether team members have technology availability or compatibility issues.

Sample Agenda for Team Destination Session:

- Orientation to the team's task, including:
  - An overview of the Team's Charter
  - An opportunity for members to react and offer suggestions about the Team's Charter
  - A review of each team member's expertise and accountabilities
- Development of team norms, technological plans, and communication plans
- Team building

Do team members understand the charter, mission, and scope of the team?

Has the team developed Team Codes and Operating Principles for behavior and team processes? For example:

- How (and how frequently) to schedule meetings
- How often e-mail and voice mail should be answered
- Etiquette for face-to-face meetings and for audio/videoconferences
- How agendas for team meetings should be developed and distributed
- Choosing who will facilitate team meetings
- Determining who is required to attend meetings
- Deciding how information and decisions will be shared following the meeting

Do team members understand their accountabilities and those of other team members? Have they agreed on accountabilities?

Has the team developed a communication plan?

Has the team determined how it will review progress?

CHAPTER 3

Context Communication: Definitions and Challenges

E ffective communication is the first of the four elements of successful virtual team performance. When interacting with others, the
more we can communicate our context, the greater the connection
and, therefore, the greater the chance of achieving the objectives that we
set out to accomplish.

The virtual workplace has transformed the business landscape
across the globe in many positive ways, but it has also altered the essence
of the human connection. As you know firsthand, connections that occur
during face-to-face exchanges become more elusive when we lose close
proximity with others.

Why is it important to foster the human connection in the virtual
world? It seems obvious that when team members share a bond they
work more productively. In the long run, building good relationships enables more effective team performance and reduces situations that are
dominated by conflict. These key benefits directly impact work product
and the organization's key deliverables.

The human connection also allows a richer path of information exchange through what I call *Context Communication*. This allows virtual
team members to understand the setting that their teammates are working in and to find the best approach to collaboration. When context is
missing, virtual teams are forced to make a greater effort to maintain the

human connection, which in turn leads to new behaviors and ways of communicating.

Let's look at two different scenarios to gain an understanding of how the multiple layers of Context Communication work and their important implications for teamwork.

Scenario A: On-Site Maria

Meet Maria, a Boston-based software consultant who works at Results Software Ltd., a firm specializing in enterprise media solutions. These days she spends much of her time running to and from meetings with her largest client, Xingo Media, an e-business publisher that develops databases for the industrial marketplace. A quick glance at her workspace shows a desk piled with paperwork (in spite of a laptop and second computer screen) and a phone that continually rings. Today is the final deadline for the deployment of Xingo's e-collaboration website, a multistage project that Maria has worked the past year to complete. Unfortunately, technical issues arise at the last minute and Maria finds herself putting out fires, tracking down their causes, and locating knowledgeable experts to fix these last-minute problems.

You know Maria because both of you have worked at Results Software headquarters in Boston for almost five years, sometimes collaborating on the same projects because she is the point person on XLB Standards. Today, at 10:00 a.m. EST, you sent her an e-mail about the launch of XLB in several satellite offices of your client, Sea-Stars Media. You need her input for tomorrow's meeting with Sea-Star's senior executives about the rollout. As she runs past you in the hallway, Maria looks stressed out. She's deep in conversation on her hands-free phone, with hot coffee in one hand, an overstuffed file in the other. Hopefully, she won't spill the coffee as she goes about her business. There's worry in her voice and you can't help but feel concerned about her deadlines.

You know from hallway chats and from the general atmosphere in the office about the demands of the Xingo Media project. Although it does not directly affect you, almost every department at Results has been involved in it at some point. Maria's promotion is dependent on the successful completion of Xingo, and you are excited that all her hard work will finally pay off. You want to find the best approach to getting Maria's timely input without distracting her from an important deadline. She walks into her office at 4:45 p.m., and you know this is her last opportunity to catch up at her desk because she always leaves at 5:00 p.m. sharp to pick up her nine-year-old twin sons from the local after-school program that ends at 5:30 p.m. Displayed throughout her office are family photos of her sons at various ages; you have met the boys and are aware of her daily routine.

If you didn't know Maria's situation so well, you might be worried about the lack of response to your e-mail; instead, you know that Maria diligently logs in remotely from home to catch up on e-mail once her children are settled after 7:00 p.m., so you are not concerned. You know she is committed to Results Software, works hard, takes on a large workload, but can always be relied on to help her teammates. Therefore, her 7:15 p.m. e-mail stating that your request will be ready by 9:30 a.m. tomorrow is no surprise.

Result: Because of your observations and background knowledge, you are not surprised that you didn't receive Maria's status update to your 10:00 a.m. e-mail until 7:15 p.m. that day, despite its "urgent" status. In fact, you could have predicted this outcome when you sent your e-mail.

Now let's look at this same situation from another vantage point—minus the visual cues, background information, personal history, shared lingo, and common understanding that you and Maria have.

Scenario B: Virtual Maria

You are a consultant with Results Software Ltd., working in the San Francisco office, so you have neither met nor spoken with Maria, who also has five years' tenure with the company. You are working on the launch of XLB for Sea-Stars Media in several of its satellite offices and were told to contact Maria today by a colleague who recommended her as the company expert on XLB Standards. So, this morning, at 10:00 a.m. EST, you e-mailed her about the launch, stating that you need her response for tomorrow's meeting with senior executives about the rollout. Because this simple request was urgent, you expected

Maria to complete it within fifteen minutes. You sent your request by 7:00 a.m. PST, to make sure it was on Maria's radar early that morning on the East Coast. By noon EST, you place a follow-up call about the e-mail. No answer. You leave a voice mail hoping that she will return the call today. By 4:00 p.m. EST, you question if Maria is still with Results Software. If she is, you wonder if perhaps an emergency arose that prevented her from responding to your request.

It is now 5:00 p.m. EST, the end of your business day, and she never answered your e-mail. Regrettably, you conclude that she will not do so today and decide on a backup plan. You do not assume that she will work beyond standard business hours.

Result: At 7:15 p.m. EST, Maria responds to your e-mail. However, by this time you dropped other work commitments and skipped a run-through of tomorrow's meeting in order to spend two hours working on a backup plan. Now, you have to discard the extra work you did and are perplexed by Maria's last-minute but welcome expertise.

The Difference?

What was the difference between scenario A and scenario B? Did Maria do anything differently? What do you know about Maria and her situation in scenario A that was not verbally communicated? Do you have the same information in scenario B? What happened because of this lack of information? What does XLB mean? Without context information you may not know what this acronym represents. If you were not familiar with Maria's personal life, what assumptions might you make when she does not respond during the business day? Without knowing her circumstances you might attribute her silence to a poor work ethic. Did she stay home—and if so, why didn't she check e-mails from there? Is she at her office? Is she even in this country or time zone? Is her phone working? Is she a responsible employee committed to the company? Is she competent, or simply overwhelmed? Who *is* Maria?

Scenario A presents a deep reservoir of background information about Maria, including her family, workload issues, schedule, work habits, personal characteristics, career goals, and hot spots in her current workday. You know her moods, concerns, caffeine levels, and more. That is a lot of information, and it helps you understand how to maintain a good working relationship. When you are aware of the other projects a team member juggles along with yours and can observe that person running to and from meetings, you are able to gauge the timing of a response. With background information it is easier to predict behavior, manage your own expectations, choose the best approach, and in general, maintain a good working relationship.

The main difference between scenario A and scenario B is *Context Communication*. In the first scenario, you know the many reasons Maria has not responded. Context had been communicated not through words, but through visual cues and shared history. Without being explicitly told, you knew when to expect a response from Maria.

What Is Context Communication?

As you can see from Maria's example, there are many different types of cues that provide information, and these layers of observable cues create context, or a sense of place. Context Communication is the framework within which we connect the dots so that they make sense. Working in the same office as our teammates allows us to observe behaviors, actions, and surroundings, creating background information from which we infer a heightened understanding of their situation. Simply put, a shared context for understanding is a given for on-site teams, and no effort is required to connect the dots because when you can see, hear, and sense cues, the dots connect themselves.

Context Communication means that team members working in close proximity can quickly assess the cues and therefore understand the context in which certain behaviors take place. Observations about another person's verbal tone, body language, and other visual cues create the context that helps us understand each other, the task at hand, and the overall work situation. Informal hallway or watercooler chats that are common with on-site teams provide a natural way to conduct casual conversations, build personal relationships, and learn additional context, some of which you store in the back of your mind for future situations.

Context Communication is achieved in three ways:

1. *Environmental Cues.* Visual, audio, and physical cues provide information about your physical surroundings, your schedule, and your workload.
2. *The Medium.* The format used for communication, such as e-mail, voice, videoconferencing, or face-to-face interactions, determines the richness of information that is communicated.
3. *Relationships.* Knowledge of teammates' personalities, career goals, friendships, alliances, and moods provides cues about work behaviors.

Let's break down the rich, multilayered information about Maria that was available in scenario A into the three types of Context Communication.

Environmental Cues

The first type of Context Communication eroded in a virtual setting is environment. The most immediate cues lost are those we take for granted in a shared office environment, such as the physical condition of the workspace, as well as visual and audio cues we get from having people around us. Context Communication cues diminish with distance, and I refer to them as *diminished cues* of the virtual environment. Virtual coworkers don't know if you are sitting at your desk, attending a meeting, or away for a particular reason. They can't see Maria running between meetings. They can't hear the phone ringing or overhear hallway chatter such as, "Did you hear about the Xingo deadline today?" When on the phone with a virtual teammate, it is not possible to know if she is doing something else, such as typing an e-mail or texting. Imagine if you couldn't hear Maria's phone continually ring (the implication being that there are many demands for her time). Imagine not knowing that a phone call might not be the best way to reach her. Unless Maria has communicated the context of her busy day, which is filled with meetings away from the office, and that she usually isn't available by phone, you may be at a loss.

There are limits to the available information about team members in the virtual space. These limits point to the three challenges faced by virtual teams due to the constraints of environmental Context Communication.

Environmental Challenge 1: Team Members' Awareness of Tasks and Availability

The on-site scenario provided evidence of Maria's busy schedule. An empty office indicated that she was at a meeting and probably couldn't call or e-mail immediately. You saw stacks of papers at her workstation, which implied a busy workday. You heard her on the phone and could see that she placed someone on hold. With so much going on you might conclude that calling might not be the best way to engage her. Next, she raced past you, indicating that she was pressed for time. Later, she returned to her office—but you knew that didn't mean she was available. At that point, you already had enough information to assess the situation, but the cues kept adding to your understanding. Certainly you conclude that Maria is not slacking off.

In addition to visual cues, you knew from past conversations that Maria spent an entire year working on a large project that was due today. You may have overheard conversations about this key project in the hallway or chatted with coworkers at lunch. Lastly, the company's intranet includes a calendar listing every current project by consultant and deadline, which is continually updated and accessed by everyone. As you can see, there are many sources of information in a nonvirtual workplace that provide rich information about Maria.

The shared calendar is more important virtually than in the on-site world because it becomes one of your few sources of context to learn about Maria's availability. However, even this calendar does not indicate interruptions and unplanned situations. Unless virtual Maria explicitly tells you about the endless stream of interruptions, you would not infer it from her calendar. Nor would you know if virtual Maria had spilled her coffee on her expensive suit and had to go to the dry cleaners next door to avoid ruining it.

Here are some practical tips to help you communicate context around tasks and availability challenges:

➤ Use group discussions and shared documents to facilitate awareness of team members' additional projects, tasks, and workload. You can add information about a team member while discussing a project. For example, you may add something like "Jason has been swamped with ABC project, so you might have to get your request in early."

➤ Share meeting calendars with teammates and keep the calendar up-to-date, even with last-minute additions.

➤ E-mail the team (and other stakeholders) if an unexpected situation makes you unavailable. You can also create standard procedures for planned situations, such as vacations, notifications, or extended trips, as well as for emergencies, to enable team members to communicate schedules and unforeseen interruptions (personal or work-related) within minutes.

➤ Ensure everyone briefly comments on what is going on in their world via a round-robin at the beginning of meetings. Giving colleagues an opportunity to talk about their issues is one way to create a habit of communicating context.

➤ Model the behavior that you want to see in others. Share social and personal information, with a rich exchange about your context, and encourage others to do the same.

Environmental Challenge 2: Lost Riders

How can you tell if someone is really working? When a team member continually pushes back deadlines, how would you know if the reasons are valid? How long does it take to detect if someone is not fulfilling her responsibilities in a virtual environment? What do you do if someone stops responding to your e-mails and phone calls, and you cannot stop by her desk? Is this team member lost, missing, or just avoiding you?

Many clients tell me that the virtual environment makes it easier for team members to hide. Some people may take advantage of the lack of daily oversight; they may get "lost" or go missing. The first clue is that deadlines are continually pushed back, and then deliverables aren't produced for days, weeks, or months. The critical time to notice situations that could lead to potential issues is during the early phase of a new project or when a new member joins the team. Also, by keeping time lines for deliverables short in the early phases, it is easier to catch problems. In fact, some clients find that short time lines work best throughout the entire life cycle of the project.

Identifying Lost Riders

➤ The individual often pushes back on deadlines, and you lack the information to verify the validity of the push-back.

➤ There's a time lag in response to e-mails and phone calls.

➤ The team member doesn't contribute work product or update reports although claims to be in meetings or on the phone most of the day working on your project.

➤ In extreme cases, a team member has seemingly stopped responding to requests.

Tips for Handling Lost Riders

➤ Have short-term goals and deliverables so that you can identify issues early.

➤ Bring issues to light as soon as you discover them. Discuss them with the team members involved.

➤ Come up with techniques to deal with people who are not responding. You can prevent this behavior by creating team Rules of the Road during the Team Setup stage, as discussed in Chapter 2. If team rules are violated, colleagues can bring up these issues as soon as they occur.

➤ Develop availability standards. Have team members state their working hours and inform others how often they check their voice mail, e-mail, and interoffice mail. And establish a standard for how quickly to respond to each mode of communication. You can publish availability standards on the team's website or in a shared system. An added advantage of availability standards is that they act as a foundation for establishing trust.

➤ Have a clear performance plan, including escalation measures, for the team. Follow through when someone becomes unresponsive or unproductive.

Be careful in labeling someone a Lost Rider. Just because someone doesn't speak up during conference calls doesn't mean she is a Lost Rider. Keep in mind that personality, hidden conflict differences, expectations about the agenda or call procedures, or cross-cultural differences are all factors that may prevent a team member from speaking up.

Environmental Challenge 3: Multitasking

One of the biggest complaints I hear regularly involves people multitasking and not truly listening. In many ways, this is the new "normal" in the business world. People often work on more than one task while conducting business calls. I met one manager who told me, "When you are in a conference room, you can see what people are doing and know if they stay engaged. On a virtual team, everyone is doing several things at once. I was expecting communication to be smoother and better understood, but I now realize that not everyone was fully participating."

Her comment made me consider the value of multitasking in the virtual environment. People appear to be listening during calls, but are they? Despite various data tools that capture caller activity during the virtual interaction, how can you tell if your virtual teammates are really listening?

Without physical (environmental) context, you can't see if your teammates are concentrating. When team members are overworked and short on time, they may feel freer to perform other tasks, like responding to e-mails, while participating on a group call. Nowadays, some online tools enable managers to see if someone is clicking on other screens or staying with the screen under discussion. The level of engagement can now be measured, and I've talked to several managers who can determine the percentage of team members actively engaged during a call. Many interviews conducted for this book noted that (1) teammates often multitask and (2) virtual managers find this behavior frustrating.

Identifying Excessive Multitasking

> The team member sounds preoccupied or has a delayed response while on a conference call.

> Background sounds are audible, which may result from keystrokes, driving in a car, or running an errand while discussing a project.

> The team member seems distracted, lost in the flow of the conversation, or asks you to repeat yourself several times. This could mean that he "checked out" of the meeting or has a bad phone connection. It could also denote cross-cultural issues, with that individual having difficulty understanding your words.

> You notice an e-mail sent from a fellow participant during a phone conference; however, that means that you too are multitasking!

Multitasking: Good, Bad, or Necessary?

A manager I recently coached said that he does not like the word *multitasking* because it has a bad connotation. He prefers to say that he "rapidly refocuses" when he handles multiple communications simultaneously. He may be an exception, or he may exemplify the new generation whose digital environment has ongoing distractions. Is that good or bad? Perhaps it is a necessary response today and going forward.

Tips for Avoiding Excessive Multitasking

> Set priorities around your team objectives to help people focus on the two or three main ones.

> Write a Team Code that details acceptable behaviors associated with multitasking, such as:

- Running errands during work hours.

- Turning off cell phone ringer/buzzer, e-mail notification, and MP3 players and tuning in during calls.

- Confronting or reminding team members who excessively multitask.

- Agreeing on when to use the "mute" button during phone conferences.

- Agreeing that certain multitasking behavior is acceptable, provided that it is done within reason. One virtual manager working for a semiconductor chip company agreed with her team that during long meetings people could work on their laptops while listening. They were not forced to participate unless something was relevant to their part of the project.

➤ Realize that multitasking is common in the virtual environment and help team members to prioritize and become fully present while on your calls by creating more urgency around deliverables.

➤ Ensure that a communication system exists to alert everyone when certain team members are participating in a scheduled conference call and therefore are unavailable to quickly respond to e-mails.

➤ Check in with teammates regularly by asking questions; for example, "How is it going on project X?" Also, get them involved in the dialogue during the call.

➤ Focus on adding value rather than adding volume. Identify activities that will truly add value to what is important and do them.

➤ Pay attention to what you can get done now.

The Medium

Medium is the second type of Context Communication; it is the format used to communicate with virtual members. Medium determines the richness of information that is received, with e-mail, phone, and videoconference the most common means of communication. But there are other ways for virtual workers to communicate, too, including using instant messaging and chat programs, whiteboards, discussion boards, file sharing, web sharing, text messages on mobile devices, and social media websites. Should you type an e-mail or send an IM? Leave a voice mail or call back? Is a videoconference better for the topic at hand? Is it better to comment on your colleague's social media site or on his blog? For a particular situation how you answer these questions will determine what you communicate and the type of response you might get.

Using Technology to Communicate

Today's technology-based contact systems offer speed and convenience as well as the ability to instantaneously communicate to large numbers of people over large distances. However, technology-based communications will always be bound by our senses, which rely upon the traditional forms of communication.

Imagine that your request to Maria about the XLB launch for Sea-Stars Media was stated in several highly detailed paragraphs. Compare that with a short, targeted e-mail with details summarized in one paragraph. Which message would better achieve your results? Although you may decide on a brief e-mail, you do not know if Maria's in-box is flooded with hundreds of messages, nor are you privy to her e-mail filters or know what keywords in the subject field would attract her immediate attention.

A variety of technological media is available to you: e-mail, text and voice messaging, electronic message boards, chat rooms, telephone conferencing, videoconferencing, and virtual file sharing. Technology is changing so rapidly that undoubtedly newer options will appear within a short time. Here, I want to review and provide practical tips for the three most popular forms of communication: written, voice, and "virtual in person."

Written Communication (E-Mail)

Electronic messaging—which includes e-mail, short message service (SMS) text, and instant messaging (IM)—is the most common virtual communication tool, but it tends to be very linear (one way) and stripped of all but the most important details. I am often amazed at how many e-mails people receive on a daily basis. People send e-mails across the cubicle or across the hall instead of walking over and having a personal interaction with their coworkers. Messages are often misunderstood and "cc:" (carbon copy) messages, in particular, become part of e-mail wars that can be defused by a simple conversation. Sometimes cleaning your in-box becomes another time-consuming task.

With technology we can do more things at once, and faster, than before, but our expectations have also expanded to meet this increased capacity. When someone sends an e-mail or text message, the expectation is an immediate response. E-mail is a double-edged sword. Although it enables easy connection, it creates human disconnection. How often do you e-mail a coworker instead of walking over to his desk or picking up the phone?

E-mail is appropriate for certain types of short updates and information sharing, such as progress reports, logistical updates, and project planning. But linear modes cannot communicate the rich contextual information that is the hallmark of same-time/same-place team interactions, like those afforded by conversing in a coworker's office or attending a live, in-person meeting.

Manage Your E-Mails or They Will Manage You! Despite potential issues with e-mail, it is universally recognized as an essential tool that is fast, efficient, and a major factor in driving the virtual workplace as a viable work arrangement. E-mail helps team members stay connected and informed, replacing snail mail for countless nuggets of information that used to be sent via letter. Information that not too long ago reached its destination in days can now be received in a fraction of a second, anytime, anyplace. However, the downside is that access to instantaneous information can cause data overload and frustration. Therefore, finding ways to manage e-mail is vital.

One option is having your team come up with e-mail filtering rules as part of your Team Code for handling messages. A sample protocol is shown in Figure 3-1.

Once the appropriate protocol is in place, consider what goes into writing an effective e-mail. The real secret is to put yourself in the place of the person receiving the message. Many writers strive to make their message as actionable as possible but fail to follow some basic principles. Based on my experience training teams to write business communications effectively, I firmly believe in the five Cs of writing: concise,

Figure 3-1. Team Code sample: e-mail protocols.

Level of Urgency: Filter e-mails with the word *Urgent* into a folder that gets checked frequently.

Level of Importance: Filter e-mails from an important stakeholder or related to a key deliverable into an "Important" folder.

Frequency: Check all other e-mails within an agreed amount of time, and respond within 24 hours.

Nature of Subject

- **For Requests:** Construct a subject line to make it searchable. A request may read, *Urgent: By 2 pm for VP: Need yesterday's sales for Product X.* Include key information, such as who needs what by when, in sufficient detail to complete the task, and be sure your callback number is part of your signature. If the response is vital, leave a short voice mail as well, as a heads-up about your request.

- **For Informational or Complex Explanations:** Call before sending. If the person is unavailable send a separate e-mail to request a telephone meeting. As an example, *Meeting Request: By 3/14. Need 15 minutes to discuss XYZ.*

complete, concrete, compact, and clear. When you construct your e-mails, keep them in mind.

Concise. Keep your e-mails short. Omit unnecessary words and avoid repetitive phrases. Especially when working with colleagues across cultures, simplify words or redundant expressions.

Complete. Your e-mails should answer essential questions: who, what, when, and if appropriate where, why, and how. By answering these questions, you can ensure that your documents satisfy the second criterion of good business writing: completeness. Complete business communications are also well organized.

Concrete. Make your writing specific, free of jargon or clichés, and use the active voice. In active voice, the person taking action appears first in the sentence and word order is more direct. For example, "I reviewed Arlene's synopsis of the marketing plan," rather than "The marketing plan that Arlene created a synopsis for was reviewed."

Compact. Limit your e-mail to short paragraphs consisting of sentences related to a single topic; keep them brief and use common words that are easy to grasp. When presenting several ideas, list items in bullet points, leaving space between paragraphs so that readers can follow your ideas.

Clear. Unlike a phone or face-to-face conversation, where people send and receive verbal and nonverbal feedback, written communication can be more problematic. Consider the following: First, you don't always receive feedback about how your e-mail is being interpreted. It is therefore possible for the reader to misinterpret what you have written and mistakenly believe that he has understood your intent. Second, once you hit "send" the message is gone and cannot be pulled back. To avoid these problems with sensitive information, write your e-mail and then wait a bit before rereading the message; put yourself in your reader's shoes before clicking "send."

Tips for Writing Effective E-Mails

➤ E-mail is subject based, so use a direct subject line that is simple, helps your reader prioritize the message, and is easy to retrieve. If the subject of your e-mail has changed, update the subject line to reflect that change.

➤ Designate priority, such as "Response Requested" or "FYI no decision required."

➤ Keep your message short and use bullets, since people increasingly receive messages on the go, on their smartphones or other mobile devices.

➤ Consider a "no scrolling" rule; that is, only include as much information as the individual can see in one screen without having to scroll down. This will force you to keep your message clear and succinct.

➤ Use headers and numbers, particularly when asking the recipient to respond to action items.

➤ Avoid writing in all capital letters unless it is an acronym; some people may interpret capital letters as yelling.

➤ Avoid making jokes or using sarcasm since this might be offensive or easily misunderstood.

➤ Update your group lists; when you receive an e-mail message as part of a group, be sure to consider whether your reply should be sent to all recipients.

➤ Don't waste people's time by copying them on everything to cover your back. If it is important to copy the person, then do it. But be aware that people can read the wrong meaning into your words and are busy themselves. Ask yourself, "Who else needs to know about this? Is it really necessary to copy them?" The answer to this question will determine if a "cc:" is needed.

➤ When forwarding an e-mail, briefly state the purpose and action required.

➤ Carefully review your message before you send it to check for and to correct potential misinterpretations.

➤ Start with "hello," not "good morning" or "good afternoon"; you won't know when the message will be read, especially for teams that follow the sun and communicate mostly by e-mail.

➤ Follow up complex e-mails with phone conversations to verify that your recipient understood the subtleties of your message. Or, have the conversation first, and then send an e-mail to confirm the conversation afterward.

Written communication requires extra care because virtual teams don't have watercooler interactions to patch things over. Before interpreting something negatively or escalating it, give the person the benefit of the doubt, and refrain from sending an angry e-mail immediately.

As a general guide you want to be extra sensitive when sending e-mails to colleagues who work remotely. A good rule of thumb: When in doubt, pick up the phone. And, if you are on the receiving end of a puzzling or troubling e-mail, call your colleague. If you feel irritated, take a deep breath and then dial the number. A short call can save hours of wasted time in writing e-mails about issues that are better conveyed in telephone conversations.

Voice Communication (Telephone)

Your voice is a powerful communication tool, and the telephone is a tried-and-true medium for "keeping in touch." On the phone, you can express your thoughts with urgency and emotion in a way that an e-mail cannot convey. The live voice remains an indispensable tool for rich and accurate communication.

Since the telephone has become such a common part of daily life, one would think that we have mastered this medium. However, that is not the case. We sometimes take for granted the ease of a phone conversation, or view its use as a necessary evil. Many virtual teams spend a good part of the workday calling each other, sometimes connecting, more often than not, leaving a message.

Voice Mail. Voice mail has an important place in virtual communication since it has the advantage of conveying the sender's tone, which adds an important dimension to Context Communication. There are specific situations where voice mail is particularly useful, such as:

> ➤ For giving status updates (either one-on-one or a group broadcast)

> ➤ To convey information that does not require a real-time conversation

> ➤ When the message is logical and brief

> ➤ When action items can be clearly stated and easily understood

Tips for Leaving a Voice Mail Message

> ➤ Keep the message structured, logical, and concise. The clearer it is, the greater the odds that the receiver will understand and respond to your message.

> ➤ Update your voice mail greeting frequently. State when you are available for a live chat, when you will return calls, and what number to call to reach a "real" person, if necessary.

> ➤ Speak clearly and slowly, especially when your teammates are from other countries.

Virtual teams can also develop a Team Code for voice mail. Some managers set these expectations and post them for the team. Figure 3-2 is an example.

Figure 3-2. Team Code for voice mail.

Acceptable Checking and Response Times: Check voice mail twice daily and respond within 24 hours.

Length of Messages: 15 seconds or less.

Purpose: Use voice mail as a quick check-in or to ask a question. Don't say it's "Urgent" unless a message needs quick response, or you will lose your credibility.

Follow-Up: Send written documentation (e-mail) when appropriate, as a follow-up to voice messages.

Call Transfers: When transferring a message, include a short explanation why you are doing so.

Conference Calls. When it is necessary for teammates to interact in real time, the conference call serves as a "live" audio channel for the virtual team. It is the quickest and easiest way to discuss strategy, review key deliverables, or brainstorm options.

> "I want to be 100 percent accessible and help my team members grow closer, because they can easily hide behind computers and not establish relationships. I take it upon myself to reach out to everyone and bring them along, learn from them, and incorporate their ideas. Each day we have the end-of-day conference call to connect, refine ideas, and plan for the next day's events."
>
> —VICE PRESIDENT OF SALES, RETAIL COMPANY

This VP understands two important concepts about conference calls: First, his leadership and initiative drive the connection; and second, without that "people" connection, the team would not work as cohesively and therefore not as productively.

Many teams have a weekly/daily morning call. Others have calls at the end of each week or each day. Some conduct calls on a certain day while others rotate them by time zone. Whatever your virtual team does, I am sure you are on numerous conference calls each day. But are they effective? Most people don't feel very positive about these calls and characterize them as frustrating experiences. They have been described to me as a "nightmare," "pointless," and "tedious."

Here are ten practical suggestions to make your conference calls more productive:

1. *Select a facilitator who can keep things moving.* The conference call facilitator is not necessarily the leader, but could be. The key is to choose someone who is a skilled facilitator rather than a lecturer or manager. You want someone with skills in group dynamics and language, and who is able to construct relevant questions and remain sensitive to balancing work issues with participants' time constraints. Consider having note-taker and timekeeper roles shared or rotated so that calls can be more efficient. And always start and end meetings on time so that people have fewer excuses to miss them.

2. *Distribute the agenda beforehand.* Treat the conference call as if it were a meeting. Prepare and distribute the agenda and any other documents pertinent to the meeting *before* the call takes place. Keep the group focused on the agenda and on the time.

3. *Identify objectives up front.* Ensure that participants are aware of the desired end results.

4. *Have ground rules in place at the beginning.* Set boundaries for everyone participating in the call by:
   - Making sure that callers say hello and introduce themselves
   - Saying your name each time you speak
   - Using your mute button to eliminate background noise
   - Focusing your comments and keeping them brief

5. *Give feedback to participants.* Tell them what they did well and where they need to shift focus. Do this halfway through if the call is not going well, or at the end if things ran smoothly.

6. *Ensure that everyone is treated with respect.* Your job as team leader and/or conference call facilitator is to protect the self-esteem of participants on the call. Facilitators should be objective, so don't criticize anyone or allow anyone else to be attacked. In addition, do not let one person dominate or hog

airtime. Keep track of who is actively participating, and engage silent individuals in the discussion.

7. *Intervene if you believe discussions are running off-track.* Nicely, but firmly, intervene if a participant is not following the ground rules. For example: "Thanks, Bart, for making that point. Let's note it for later since it's not part of today's agenda."

8. *Maximize the entire group's input.* Be sure to get everyone involved. If you deem the call necessary and useful, make sure it is an interactive experience for everyone. Otherwise, ask yourself if the day's business could just as easily be conducted in a series of e-mails.

9. *Debrief at the end.* Ask members whether they found the meeting valuable. Did it match your agenda and meet the intended outcomes? Conclude the call as you would any meeting, summarizing, confirming decisions, and reiterating future steps.

10. *Evaluate before planning the next teleconference.* Was every participant essential? Could the issues have been handled by e-mail? Was this precious time used to brainstorm, resolve differences, and make decisions? Make sure everyone's time was well spent.

Conference Calls and Silent Riders. It is easy for team members to stay in the background and impassively witness a conversation in e-mail strings and conference calls. In the virtual workplace, a lack of contribution is less noticeable than at on-site meetings. Even motivated team members may be quiet during these times. I refer to colleagues who do not contribute during conference calls as Silent Riders. Silent Riders may fulfill their responsibilities but may need an extra push to join the discussion. To encourage quiet team members to speak up, you may need to try several approaches. Ask questions to keep the conversation alive. Or you can do a round-robin to hear from every attendee. Alternatively, you can occasionally ask a specific participant a question ("Alex, what do you think?").

If you are dealing with global language barriers, Silent Riders may need an extra nudge. One of my clients, a virtual manager at an international insurance conglomerate, had to conduct regular conference calls with ten people from five different countries in Asia. During his first call, few team members spoke, and he found the added difficulties of language barriers and background noise made it even more difficult to communicate. Together we came up with these guidelines to draw out his Silent Riders.

1. Keep things simple (language, structure, process).

2. Send handouts ahead of time.

3. Conduct meetings with a high degree of facilitation.

4. Tightly structure the meeting, using one or more of the following techniques:

    a. Set priority. Is the meeting high or low priority? Make sure you ask because participants may not speak up.

    b. Ask people to talk about two things that are going well and two things that are not.

    c. Practice "back briefing" by asking participants to paraphrase what they heard/understood.

    d. Use a scale (like the Likert 1 to 5 scale) when framing questions to draw people out and get them to make decisions. For example, "Do you think XYZ is a 4 or 5?" That is, get people to say whether they agree or strongly agree with XYZ issue. Simple questions help Silent Riders speak up and stay involved in the discussion.

I like the saying "None of us is as smart as all of us." Keep that saying in front of you as a reminder that the results of encouraging more reticent team members are worth the extra effort of engaging them. In addition, you cannot assume that every member on the call has all the relevant information, since the team is a fluid entity, with members leaving and arriving because of ongoing projects and commitments. Also, consider the kinds of questions that new team members participating in their first call might have. For instance:

➤ Were important points about the topic made on previous calls? (In other words, what is the history of an ongoing conversation?)

> ➤ What is this call supposed to accomplish?

> ➤ Who is responsible for specific agenda items and who is knowledgeable about key issues?

> ➤ Do I know what our team's specific acronyms and shorthand mean?

Conference calls are indispensable for moving complex projects along. It is up to you, the manager, to create the context for meeting attendees to connect the dots to the bigger picture and drive your team success.

Virtual In-Person Communication (Video and Web Conferences)

It is commonly stated that when delivering a message, the impact on others is as follows: Voice accounts for 38 percent of the impact, and the actual message just 7 percent; however, visual impression delivers 55 percent of total impact. There is no substitute for eye contact. And of all mediums currently available in the virtual world, videoconferences most closely simulate live meetings. They enable participants to see one another, as if they are in the same room, which helps to foster relationships and mutual trust in the virtual space. Videoconferences can be used to introduce new team members. They are also highly useful when teams need to *see* a mechanical object in motion (e.g., how a prototype of a new product works), various package designs, or a sales presentation. Thanks to advances in technology, today's video equipment produces high-quality images and is reliable and affordable. There are low-cost webcams that can easily be set up to record activity, as well as better-quality camera systems that integrate video, voice, data, and a web interface. By logging on to the same website, colleagues from several locations can participate in a videoconference. Once the meeting is under way, other "virtual in-person" tools are available, such as whiteboards, electronic walls, and interactive software.

Several large companies, like IBM, consider videoconferencing a vital tool in the virtual world. And, throughout the interviews conducted to research this book, most virtual managers expressed a positive view of videoconferencing capability and interest in using it more often to build human interactions, particularly in light of smaller travel budgets. By and large, the managers agreed that videoconferences afford their teams these benefits: a closer connection than conference calls, the ability to conduct unstructured conversations, and an economical way to simulate live conversation.

Future communication mediums are moving toward creating a workplace that, in spirit and feel, is as close as possible to live, in-person meetings. Here are some tips for getting the most out of your videoconference:

1. *Test the working conditions of your equipment.* Do it before any important conference.

2. *Make sure you are in a quiet location.* You want to minimize or eliminate disturbances. Don't shuffle papers, scrape your chair, tap your pencil, hum, or do other distracting, noisy activities.

3. *Have a set of simple guidelines in place for all videoconferences.* For better or worse, team members can't hide on camera. Since you don't want anything to interfere with the purpose of the meeting itself, good manners and appropriate behavior are important. Keep your guidelines simple. They should be easy to follow and easy to remember. For example, look at the camera, don't fidget, speak into the microphone clearly and slowly, and pause frequently.

4. *Remind participants of these guidelines early in the session.* The facilitator or moderator should advise participants of the basic rules of the videoconference before general interaction begins. This includes both general etiquette and any specific rules the moderator deems necessary.

5. *Begin on time, stick to the agenda, and end on time, thereby allowing participants to keep other commitments.* If you gain a reputation for running meetings efficiently, then fewer participants will be no-shows or drop out of the meeting prematurely. It is helpful for the conference's host to arrive a few minutes early to greet each participant. That way you can head off any premature discussions participants may engage in before everyone is in place.

6. *Have all participants say hello and introduce themselves.* After all expected participants are in view, the moderator should introduce each person and briefly state the person's responsibilities on the call. This is especially true if there are guests or newcomers on the call. Even though you may never meet in person, it's a good relationship builder and gets the shyest of people to at least say their name.

Web Conferences. Today, web conferences are commonplace because of the ease of the technology. Attendees join a web conference by clicking on a link (invitation) in an e-mail or web page, or by downloading an application on their computers that gives them access to additional tools (e.g., whiteboard, chat, polling, and breakout rooms). These features allow you to get a pulse on who is contributing what.

What techniques can you use in a web conference to ensure that all attendees are engaged? From facilitating these types of conferences I have learned that the basis of a successful meeting is to set the expectation up front that all attendees are expected to participate. By signing on as separate users, everyone can engage in the features offered by web conferences.

If there are newcomers to your web conference, spend an extra minute helping these attendees feel comfortable. If the web conference is a large one, set up a brief preconference walk-through. You will find that those who take you up on this offer will appreciate this extra attention, and you will be rewarded with a fully present attendee.

During the meeting use all the tools at your disposal, and make sure that everyone knows how to use them. Brainstorming can occur using chat. Paired chat is another option, where team members are paired up in a short brainstorming assignment. Polls provide an easy electronic record of key discussions, and during a debrief, the top answers to your polls or surveys can become your action plan.

Guidelines for Maximizing Participation in a Video or Web Conference

> ➤ Ask all participants for agenda items and distribute the agenda before the meeting.

Teleconference: A conference in which participants in different locations communicate with each other via a telephone (audio only) call.

Videoconference: A conference in which participants use video and audio transmissions simultaneously through a live connection. At its simplest, participants view static images and graphics; at its most sophisticated, participants experience full-motion video images and meet virtually in person.

Web Conference: A conference that is hosted via the World Wide Web. Participants see the same screen at all times in their Web browsers. Some Web-conferencing systems include texting and VoIP (Voice Over IP).

➤ Make sure all technical tools are set up before the meeting.

➤ When the conference begins, identify yourself (as host or facilitator) and briefly mention the names of everyone who is present and introduce anyone who is new. Make sure to clearly note when anyone enters or departs from the conference session.

➤ Pause at regular intervals; ask for others' views and/or questions.

➤ Refrain from behavior that could alienate participants, such as long monologues or extended conversations with people sitting next to you.

➤ Look into the camera when speaking, not at people sitting in the same room.

➤ Be aware of lag time, and don't jump to new points, which may confuse listeners.

➤ Make sure that main points are summarized and action items are clearly stated and then distributed to each participant.

Relationships

Relationships are the third type of Context Communication. They are the glue that holds team members together. To overcome the difficulties of working across physical distances, relationships need to be constructed using tools (e.g., telephone and/or computers) that were not designed to build relationships.

After the initial Team Setup phase, you still need to develop team relationships, as members continue to learn about their teammates' personalities, work styles, moods, friendships, and career goals. Without the opportunity to lunch with colleagues, it's up to you, as team leader, to build relationships by creating the missing social elements in different ways. Relationships create the social communication context from which you can infer information about your teammates.

How do virtual managers foster critical relationships? The overwhelming message sent by people who walk in your shoes is to find a way to build the relationship with your team. From a leader perspective, be accessible, reach out, and connect with your virtual team:

> "You have to build relationships with people you don't see, and you need them more than they need you. No one will do it for you. So force yourself to call everyone on your team; maintain relationships, because if you are out of sight you are out of mind for a lot of people. It's not comfortable. But I make sure I do it."
>
> —MANAGER, CONSUMER ELECTRONICS COMPANY

> "I make sure that I am 100 percent accessible and I help my employees along because in virtual teams, people tend to hide behind computers, and you are not going to establish relationships via e-mail. So I reach out to them and bring them along. I learn from them and incorporate their ideas. My biggest value-add is being 100 percent accessible."
>
> —GLOBAL MOBILITY MANAGER, CREDIT CARD COMPANY

Recall Maria's situation, as set out earlier in this chapter. In scenario A, you worked in the same office as Maria and observed her personality, work ethic, moods, and personal commitments. In scenario B, you had to infer cues about virtual Maria. Let's say virtual Maria wants to establish better connection with her teammates and develop better work relationships. She must overcome the three relationship context challenges: (1) isolation, (2) personality, and (3) history.

Relationships Challenge 1: Isolation

"I'm on my own island. I'm by myself," a virtual leader at an information solutions company told me. Let's call him the Islander. He said, "I need to figure things out by myself." The Islander was unaware of what teammates were doing and felt like he worked in a vacuum. "I'm on conference calls," he said, "and I don't know what anyone looks like or who they are. I met my first manager, but not my second or third manager. The most information I can get about teammates is their online profile or résumé, but it doesn't even have a picture. It doesn't tell me very much about who they are."

He goes on to describe his communication challenges: "It's easy to be in your own world since you don't have quick sidebar conversations as you would in the office. All communication is behind e-mails, and I have no idea how things work. E-mails can be misread, and it's hard to know if something cool is happening in the company because there is no visibility."

When asked about relationships with his immediate team, he describes his interactions as follows: "If you are not there, people don't know you. In an office people can see you and know what you're doing. There's something about going into someone's office and talking about what's going on—have a conversation, agree and shake hands. I miss that. When you are out there alone, people have no clue what's going on and they can forget you."

The Islander's situation summarizes two main problems regarding the isolation that can occur in virtual teams: the need for managers to build working relationships with their team, and the need to engage team members with each other when a sense of team is lacking.

Most of the time, isolation is associated with feeling disconnected from teammates because of the lack of personal interaction or social connection after work hours. Many people hope to attend an occasional in-person meeting, budgets permitting; they believe that interacting face-to-face every few months helps build relationships. Despite the cost factor, many people point out that face time is critical.

If face time is eliminated, or drastically reduced, what can you do to bring together your Islanders and assemble your castaways? How can you facilitate the human connection in this virtual world? What tools are at your disposal to pull your team together and build relationships so that people feel connected?

Your greatest contribution as a virtual leader is to *find that connection* with people and keep it alive, because the human factor is still the most powerful element in our virtual world. Shortly, we will explore ways to do that.

Relationships Challenge 2: Personality

> "I wish that when I started, somebody did an overview with me of the personalities involved, because it takes so long to know the people. If you want this person to do something, you have to do X. For another person, you need a totally different approach. So-and-so only wants a one-sentence summary to approve budgets. Personality differences take a long time to learn because there's so much disparity in how people like to do things. Everybody has their own preference. I have to figure out what's going to work with each person."
>
> —MANAGER, INTERNATIONAL NONPROFIT ORGANIZATION

Let's return to Maria, that hardworking consultant. She's a diligent, responsible project manager whom you have counted on in the past. Knowing her personality, work patterns, and preferences helps you determine the best approach in terms of how (communication medium) and when (time of day) it is best to reach her. You do not have to waste time wondering where Maria is, if and when she will contact you, since you know she checks e-mails during the evening. If your request isn't clear, Maria will call to discuss her questions. There would be no need to plan a backup scenario.

Now, let's return to your virtual world. Although it is important to be sensitive to others' styles in all work situations, for virtual teams it often means the difference between a frustrating and a rewarding relationship. How can you learn about your teammates' work style, preferences, and personality when you don't have opportunities to observe them in person? Let's say you work with Walter, who has communicated several times that he prefers all the information up front, even if the e-mail is long. When you inadvertently omitted some details about your request he was clearly annoyed, although he did not call you for clarification (Walter claims to be allergic to the phone!). If you work on projects for Maria and him, how can you adapt to their different behavioral cues? Besides handling the Team Setup phase well, what can you do? As the manager, an important part of your role is to create social knowledge so that team members learn each other's preferences.

Relationships Challenge 3: History

Virtual teams regularly share data files, information, and updates, but do they share history? With team members often joining and departing midway through projects, history becomes difficult to capture. It is hard enough to learn the team's lingo, norms, and communication styles. Now there are past experiences to be aware of and remember. Think about a good childhood friend of yours, someone you grew up with, or with whom you shared something meaningful. A bond was formed, and when your friend calls, you often smile to yourself. No question you would go the extra distance for this person if asked. That type of connection doesn't exist with virtual teammates. Nevertheless, creating shared experiences can open communication lines to increase understanding. Your shared history will motivate your colleagues to help you and to let them know that you can be counted on as well.

As a manager, one of your jobs is to create the conditions for contact to deepen into history—and that requires regular contact between people so they can make and grow work-related connections. The secret sauce to overcoming isolation in the virtual world is to create what I call a *virtual watercooler*.

The Virtual Watercooler

There are many ways to create interactions that replicate on-site office environments, where people meet each other in break rooms, chat near the coffee machine, celebrate birthdays, and have watercooler conversations. Without the luxury of face time, you can simulate creative gatherings to connect your team members to each other and to you.

Here are suggestions for how virtual teams can create the virtual water-cooler for themselves:

Getting to Know Each Other

- Kick off a conference call with a Welcome Party when new members join.

- Have team members share their pictures with a quote (or motto) that describes something about them *before* your meeting. Then provide a bit of time to socialize at the beginning of the call—just enough time to create a friendly atmosphere.

- Set up a "get to know everyone" virtual gathering and discuss business challenges.

- Establish a team website that gives your team an identity and includes members' photos, bios, and personal information. Some companies are creating an internal social network across their organization (think of it as a proprietary Facebook). Use your internal network to share information, updates, and announcements via social media sites preferred by your team.

Building Rapport During Meetings

- Include time for social discourse so that members can make natural connections. For example, a team in the financial services industry conducts a timed five-minute "check-in" conversation at the start of calls and then individuals follow up by phoning each other between meetings.

- Assign "break buddies" who can chat with each other after the team call or during a break.

- Encourage perspective sharing. During team updates, ask attendees to state their perspective on an issue so that team members can better understand each other's values and styles.

- Conduct a brainstorming call. Use a round-robin technique and solicit everyone's input. Follow collaborative brainstorming guidelines that encourage "No judgment" and "Listening."

- During larger meetings and with larger teams, use the whiteboard to write attendees' locations or display a world map so that people can see each other's name, location, and time of day.

- Rotate the schedule for conference calls so that the discomfort of participating at inconvenient times doesn't fall on one party or one time zone.

Creating Ongoing Social Interactions

- Get team members to talk about their family or pets, to share something of themselves.

- Treat everyone with respect and as a potential friend. Learn one thing about each team member's life outside of work—an interest or special hobby, for instance.

- Discover tricks to build rapport across the divide: Pay attention to holidays in different countries and send e-cards or short communications to wish your teammates "happy holidays" in their language.

- Reach out to teammates you haven't heard from and say, "We haven't talked; do you want to sync up or check in for ten minutes?" Usually they will be willing to meet you halfway.

- Learn your teammates' IM habits and send quick texts. One interviewee from an electrical distribution company told me that she noticed her teammate's IM at 11:00 p.m., so she wrote back, "You need to go to sleep to keep that beautiful complexion," and they both laughed (-: virtually :-).

Adding Some Fun

- Have a virtual team-building session where everyone plays video games with each other.

- Use flash cards for playing cards online.

- Give a virtual "pat on the back" by sending a recognition e-mail to your teammate.

- Exchange favorite recipes during the holidays. Pick a holiday and explore its traditions (food, dress, customs) for a few minutes during your call so that teammates learn about its cultural relevance.

- Have a virtual pizza party. Send pizza to each location at the same time; then get together on the call or via an Internet chat session to "chew and chat."

- Orchestrate a virtual surprise party. One manager at a credit card company became the famous chocolate lady when she coordinated a surprise birthday party for a colleague in London. She arranged for local members to provide cake and flowers and sent Russian chocolates to everyone. The surprise party took place during the team's weekly call, and even the managing director stopped in the office to offer birthday wishes. They took pictures and e-mailed them to everyone on the team. I was told that this party helped the team bond and was talked about for months.

- Provide a virtual break room. Encourage teammates to use social media tools to share information, insights, and even news. Agree on guidelines and policies for appropriate use.

- Create a forum for team members to create their own social networks around sports teams, television shows, or other events. Have users share updates, rankings, quizzes, and opinions, thus encouraging interaction. Moderators can be rotated on an ongoing basis.

- When a project ends, ask teammates to send you pictures to share with everyone. One such team at a software company sent pictures to the sponsor, who created a picture gallery, framed it, and sent it to every member. Everyone felt recognized and positive about the experience.

Find Your Rhythm

All teams, virtual or not, fall into routines. These routines can lead to a comfortable operating rhythm, which forms the pulse of a high-functioning unit. You can help develop this rhythm by pushing for regular communications. Think of yourself as a concert conductor who leads the orchestra, making sure that the music flows at just the right tempo or rhythm. That means helping those who feel isolated find the connection, working to build their social knowledge, and creating the conditions for isolated events to become shared history.

The Link Between Context Communication and Accountability

Good communication unites your team. And creating the context for shared understanding is one of your key tasks. Complete the Virtual Roadmap exercise at the end of this chapter, which is written as a series of questions, to once again reflect on the multiple layers of Context Communication. Think about your own team as you consider the questions in the Virtual Roadmap and use them to frame appropriate communication mechanisms to enhance your virtual context.

A virtual team is like any community in that its culture is a product of common norms and ongoing interactions that lead to shared experiences. Team members may not verbalize it, but they look to you to provide opportunities that make this happen. When context is communicated well, it builds accountability and trust, without which teams fail to achieve superior performance. As you will see in the next chapter, trust is based on experience, reputation, and reliability.

YOUR VIRTUAL ROADMAP TO CONTEXT COMMUNICATION

Environmental Cues	Medium	Relationships
• What is your organization's attitude toward virtual work?	• What technology formats are used for communications?	• What is the greatest challenge faced by your virtual team members? What about virtual managers?
• How do your organization's values support or oppose virtual work?	• How well does your infrastructure support virtual collaboration?	• What are the human constraints or supports on your team? What human support systems are in place?
• What environmental cues provide information about your surroundings, your schedule, and your workload?	• How does your infrastructure handle network connection issues?	• Do team members know about each other's personalities, work styles, and priorities?
• What is the overall leadership or communication style your team embraces?	• What mechanisms are in place for information sharing and easy access?	• Have team members shared information about their roles?
• How well is the local and virtual office designed to accommodate additional team meeting spaces?	• Is the right medium matched with the right message?	• What are you doing to foster human connection across your team?
	• Do team members know how to fully utilize virtual communication tools and collaborative software? Do they need technical support?	• Have you established a framework so that friendships, alliances, and rapport can occur?

CHAPTER 4

Developing Accountability in a Virtual World

A ccountability is like the fuel flowing through the engine of the team. It is the essential bond that enables the team to operate successfully. Team members must have faith in their colleagues' ability to deliver. This is true for all types of teams, and even more so in the virtual world, where bonds are more fragile. Without accountability, a virtual team will most likely fragment and not fulfill its goals. Without accountability in the virtual environment it is difficult, if not impossible, to carry on.

But what exactly is accountability? How is it tied to factors that make the team function or, lacking these factors, perform poorly?

Simply put, accountability is the act of taking responsibility for one's actions, and accepting the consequences if predetermined goals are not met. Much like the term *virtual team,* people have their own definitions for what accountability means to them.

The definitions of accountability that follow are taken from various client conversations about this subject and from VT managers interviewed for this book.

Accountability Is About *You*

"Accountability starts with yourself—you need to hold yourself accountable for your own deliverables. Once others see that you are committed to your own accountability, and meet deadlines, they will trust you. People who take pride in their work and have higher standards for themselves and are accountable for their actions become trustworthy."

—VT MANAGER, MAJOR ACCOUNTING FIRM

Accountability Is About Clarity

"Clarity and transparency are key. Today, we have an organization that is divided into subgroups, and it is clear who needs to handle what aspects of the job. At the beginning, people felt they would get more work and didn't want to take on responsibility for [figuring out] 'who is doing what.' Then I did the organizational transition, and now the organization is clearer—each person knows his role and is accountable for it."

—SENIOR GLOBAL LEADER, MANUFACTURING

Accountability Is About Influence

"Accountability is challenging because people work on multiple team arrangements and the team leader is not necessarily [their direct] supervisor. So influence skills—building shared commitments and practices—become important. In my team, I created a directory where people share information about what they are doing, their deadlines, and whether they are on track. We have a task checklist, and the virtual manager serves as the task coordinator. If we have a strong mission and purpose, people have a greater sense of responsibility. It all comes down to influence skills."

—VT MANAGER, BANKING

Accountability Is About Operational Rhythm

"It goes back to having standard routines about communication and operations, and it becomes part of everything you do. For example, if you have a team meeting every Tuesday at 11:00 a.m., and every other Monday [there is] a 9:30 a.m. meeting with your boss—this becomes part of your weekly rhythm. Routine should be transparent and the vehicle [technology] is different depending on your need."

—VT LEADER, BOTTLING COMPANY

Accountability Is About Performance

"My team members are all 'remote' and 'virtual,' but report to me. I keep them on target. Some are very organized and clear on accountability. Others need more guidance. In any virtual organization, it is very important to know who is accountable—when, how long, and how much.

—SENIOR VT LEADER, MEDICAL TECHNOLOGY COMPANY

Accountability Is About Culture

"There are some cultures where they take less responsibility. That's easy because there's a process. There are target dates. We have weekly meetings to discuss the status and due dates."

—VT MEMBER, TELECOMMUNICATIONS COMPANY

Clearly, accountability is one of the most important aspects of working on a team because it leads to team effectiveness. This is true for both on-site and virtual teams. It is even more applicable in the virtual environment because the true measurement of each team member's success is the person's individual contribution to the group's efforts. And, without visual cues to create the context that allows someone to tell whether another person is actively engaged in a task at a given time (e.g., observations of the person's facial expressions, body language, or other activities), virtual teams rely heavily on results against promises. Many studies conducted on virtual teams have found that personal accountability is rated as one of the most important factors in a successful virtual team. In fact, the characteristic associated most often with virtual team success is *individual and mutual accountability*. In other words, it doesn't matter whether members are all "remote" or "virtual"; what matters most is staying on target and being clear on what each member is truly responsible for achieving.

Creating Accountability in a Virtual Environment

How can you create accountability on your virtual team? Fortunately, there are many best practices from experienced virtual managers—

working managers like yourself. Here are some of their practical suggestions. As you read this list, choose a few items that resonate with your situation, and try them out with your own team:

➤ Get senior support from the beginning.

➤ Solicit people who have subject matter expertise (SME) and know what is involved.

➤ Make sure your people have the authority to make decisions.

➤ Be clear in your communications: Clarity creates commitment!

➤ Set expectations up front regarding what needs to be achieved and who does what (i.e., have a clear definition of ownership) and provide deadlines so that everyone knows and is committed.

➤ Have each person's or each subteam's deadlines roll up to the multiple-page plan.

➤ Conduct regular reporting on tasks: Are they done? If not, why not?

➤ Have regular successive meetings set on the calendar even if you don't have much to talk about.

➤ Conduct one-on-one (1:1) meetings where you can ask the "softer" questions: What needs to be done? Who did it today? If delayed, why? What help do you need? How is that XYZ report we need coming along? What problems are you having with it?

➤ Check results regularly and create a feedback loop. Some virtual teams give daily status reports while other teams send e-mails at the end of the day to review progress (e.g., What did you do today and what do you plan on doing tomorrow?).

➤ Make one person own a core responsibility. Organize due dates around that person and make sure the person reports back.

➤ Create a "share point" on the Internet or a "shared drive" on your servers, or find another tool that helps everyone stay informed and share data (e.g., folders and work files).

> ➤ Integrate work tools to help clarify ownership on projects and enable virtual teams to make decisions quickly as business needs change.

> ➤ If and when things don't work out, don't hide or blame someone else. Take responsibility; jump in and raise your hand.

Accountability is about getting things done and following through. But setting guidelines for accountability becomes even more important for virtual teams because clarity creates commitment. And commitment creates dependability. Dependability builds trust, and behind accountability is trust, the energy that sustains the entire operation. Trust is the foundation upon which accountability sits. And trust develops when team members realize that other members are reliable and can be held accountable. So, if you say you are going to do something, do it!

−−−CASE STUDY

Flagging Down Accountability

Because of a multitude of errors, one of my retail clients lost revenue. As the errors kept occurring, managers tracked mistakes on the basis of their frequency, need for escalation, and quality of initial customer contact. Not surprisingly, finger-pointing ensued. The situation was grim: Key customer orders were not completed because people "forgot" certain important items or thought that other teams or other parts of the organization were responsible for those orders. Deadlines were missed and profits suffered. At one critical juncture several items were not ordered and ready in time for holiday shipments. Cross-functional teams scattered and scrambled to get local vendors to help, but the loss of time, money, and trust created a huge gap.

Finding themselves at the end of their rope, the managers reached out for tools to help clarify accountability, create ownership, and rebuild trust in their organization. They chose a project management tool that created greater accountability among the team. Through this tool all team members must keep track of their own responsibilities using a Flag system, which consists of placing markers on all ongoing projects indicating dates and time lines for review. The Flags indicate the following:

Red Flag—We need to regroup into crisis mode when issues come up.
Yellow Flag—We are a little nervous about a deadline.
Green Flag—Project steps are on target.

With this new system in place ownership became clearer and finger-pointing diminished. Now each team was aware of its own impact on the bottom line and where its projects affected other workers' deliverables. Supplies were ordered in advance, work was performed more efficiently, and responsibility became transparent. During subsequent meetings, everyone had visibility and shared the same template and work product. With Flags clearly indicating workflow issues, everyone viewed the same data simultaneously and received complete status updates. And, at the same time, the Flag system enabled management to hold people accountable and catch any mistakes or slips as they were occurring rather than after the fact. Team members took on a greater role in reporting and used conference calls to update each other on external partner issues.

As my client said, "This tool opened up discussions and [let us keep] an 'ear to the ground' to know what's going on out there. Everyone knew what they were accountable for, and key updates occurred. I learned that for accountability and trust to occur, we needed to keep things simple, shared, and straightforward."

Accountability and Trust . . .

It is impossible to overstate the importance of trust and accountability in business (as with all human) relationships. Accountability and trust are spoken of in the same breath because they are interrelated. Accountability provides the energy for the virtual team's day-to-day activities, but trust is the larger concept and at the very core of human interactions. And trust develops over time.

In the virtual environment, trust develops once team members realize that their teammates are reliable. When team members complete an activity they have committed to, trust is built. Acting responsibly is important for all teams, but it is even more critical within virtual teams because they are working across distance, time, and space. My consulting experience with various global clients and their virtual operations has introduced me to something called "swift" or "instant" trust. This kind of trust is very important for virtual success, and yet it is hard to establish because virtual team members do not share long tenures together, and they lack the face-to-face communication and team-building opportunities that normally elicit trusting relationships.

Because virtual teams may work on short-term assignments and move on to new projects quickly, Instant Trust is extremely important on the road to building Lasting Trust. In this environment, teams often form and disband quickly, so trust has to be built almost immediately. To build Instant Trust, members must quickly establish a reputation for performing tasks and acting with integrity; they need to develop reliability and accountability. Simply stated, through accountability, people act trustworthy, which leads to Lasting Trust.

Road to Lasting Trust

Instant Trust

Often virtual teams are formed without members ever meeting. Due to business demands, these teams must hit the ground running and develop a way of working and quickly establishing trust. In these instances teams forgo team building and are forced to instantly trust each other and form instant "blind faith" relationships that place emphasis on doing and involving, rather than relating to each other.

Accountability

Accountability is the fuel that springs from trust; think of it as a critical element that flows throughout the engine of the team. It is hard to work with people who are not accountable, and if you do not find people to be accountable, then it is not possible to perceive them as trustworthy. Many of the activities that are used to build trust are activities that are necessary in building accountability as well, such as sharing information and speaking up when something is not clear.

Lasting Trust

Lasting Trust is developed when an individual's actions are predictable. Based on someone's work history, assumptions are made as to the person's reliability. If the individual has consistently delivered, then colleagues can reasonably predict that this behavior will continue. However, if someone shows a lack of consistency, then trust will be diminished.

Trust is extremely important because it creates a place for people to interact and connect with each other. Those connections—similar to the axles on the wheels of a car—enable teams to function efficiently and develop long-term relationships.

Trust is necessary for the team dynamics to function properly. Of course, having a competent leader who picks reliable people and provides critical resources is important as well. When trust is broken, then colleagues no longer turn to each other for assistance or work closely; ultimately, the unit breaks down and individuals go off on their own. This situation occurs more readily in the virtual environment where the majority of tasks are worked on individually.

Trust—Hard to Build, Easy to Break!

Figure 4-1 shows what happens to a team when there is trust and no trust. Without trust, we are less honest, and less willing to collaborate

Figure 4-1. Trust creates teamwork.

Trust	No Trust
Shared responsibility	Individuality
Shared information	Conflict
Shared ideas	Inefficiency
Shared participation	Divergent results
Shared goals	Information hoarding
Shared tasks	Miscommunication

and openly communicate; instead, energy is spent on self-protective measures. We keep ourselves at a distance, observing rather than participating. We resort to withholding, withdrawal, persuasion, or argumentation. Trust is a measure of our well-being, our ability to live more honestly, to be open to learning and participating without holding back.

Fear brings about defenses and stops a positive communication flow. We put on masks to get ahead or to get along for the short term. Fear also creates dangerous situations because we become defensive and sometimes produce exactly the outcomes we feared. Progress is not made when we surround ourselves with worry or allow others to direct us through their defensive strategies.

You've heard the saying: *Trust brings trust. Fear brings fear.* Trust and fear are the keys to understanding people. Your trust level at any given moment determines how open, personal, and independent you will be. Simple to say, harder to practice. . . .

> ➤ Trust starts with vulnerability and continues with acceptance.

> ➤ Trust involves being open to experience, taking risks, putting fears aside, and being transparent. It means being honest with oneself and open to building trusting relationships.

> ➤ Behaving authentically and showing true feelings produces trust. Withholding, rationalizing, depersonalizing, and reading into behaviors ("Why are they doing what they are doing?") feed fear, cynicism, and distrust. It doesn't take long for this to happen, and the effect is powerful.

> ➤ To get trust, you must give trust. Treat others with dignity, courtesy, and equality and appreciate people with different backgrounds, cultures, and ideas.

> ➤ Despite wonderful advances in technology and its possibilities regarding synchronous communications, the foundation of all human connections is contingent upon trust.

> ➤ Business is conducted through relationships, and trust is about relationships—and only those who are open with information about their thoughts, ideas, and feelings earn high levels of trust in relationships.

> ➤ Trust is about creating a nonhierarchical status of equality and interpersonal respect.

> ➤ Trust is about creating synergy.

> ➤ Trust is about driving collaboration.

> ➤ Trust is about enabling connection.

Trust is difficult for most people. Human beings, especially adults, desire self-preservation. Putting themselves at risk for the good of the others is not something that comes naturally, and it is rarely rewarded.

Think about things we learn from a very young age; comments such as, "Look out for number one" or "Don't let them see you suffer." It's no wonder we naturally learn to think of ourselves before others.

The key to building trust is to get comfortable being exposed to other people as vulnerable, and being unafraid to say "I was wrong," "I am not sure," or "I need help," and, yes, even saying "I am sorry." If team members cannot bring themselves to say these words when the situation calls for it, then they aren't going to learn to trust one another and will waste time and energy thinking *What should I say?* and wondering about everyone else's true intentions.

So, start small. . . . Get comfortable with moderate vulnerability.

One rule above all guides virtual team behavior, and it is especially vital when team members haven't met in person and so they cannot pick up the nonverbal signals inherent in face-to-face communication. The rule is: *Assume positive intent of your teammates.* Simply, give others the benefit of the doubt.

Building Trust Starts with You

Your most important task is to build trust. Therefore, your key role as a *chief trust leader* (CTL) is to build trust in you, in the project, and in a unified team, despite the challenges of distance, time, and space. Make sure that communication is strong enough to defeat the obstacles of geography, isolation, and history. It is communication that enables us to build the trust we need for success. Only when trust flourishes do people do magically wonderful things together!

Leadership is no longer perceived as power and control over people. Twenty-first-century leadership is even more important, exciting, and challenging. It starts with giving away power, giving people the *benefit of positive intent,* and giving up some of your guard to demonstrate vulnerability.

And like any good relationship (friendship, marriage, partnership), trust within a team is never complete; it must be maintained over time. In fact, many people claim that trust is the single most important driver for the success of virtual teams. Once trust is established, it is possible to gain consensus, build agreements, and influence others in your direction.

Think about your own experiences on virtual teams. A natural part of any relationship is the building or the breaking of trust.

During the early stages of a team's development it is helpful to do the following exercise: Ask everyone to list the behaviors they associate with building trust and ones they associate with breaking trust. Then conduct a discussion about what are the most important goals for them to achieve on this team, and what trust behaviors they agree to hold each other accountable for. This is an exercise I often do in my training workshops, but you can also present it during a conference call and engage in a productive dialogue.

Figure 4-2 is a list of behaviors that build trust and those that break trust within organizations. Take the time before you continue reading to consider your own ideas in the two areas. Later in this chapter there are several best practices and success tips for developing long-lasting trusting relationships.

As a manager, remember that trust does not occur in a vacuum. Feedback messages are more effectively heard and acted upon when offered in an environment of mutual trust. In a virtual setting, your behaviors have a particularly strong impact on that environment.

Team members often tell me that they want a virtual manager to have human "value" characteristics such as honesty, loyalty, respect, and commitment. They often say things like, "I want my boss to share information," or "I want my boss to help us create common goals and make sure we all value the same things," or "I want my manager to

Figure 4-2. Trust-building and trust-breaking behaviors.

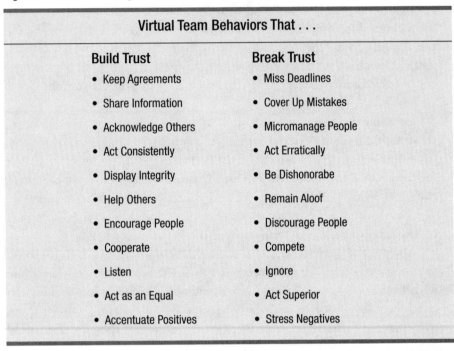

show emotional support and be someone whom I can depend upon when I need to." Virtual managers tell me that they look for team members who get done what they promised on time, and who demonstrate emotional stability and integrity and are motivated to succeed.

What are the most common trust breakers on virtual teams according to my conversations with clients? Those that involve missing deadlines, not "keeping in touch," keeping information private, being "secretive" (avoiding), making excuses, and delaying results. These breakdowns happen more often in the virtual environment because the face-to-face element is missing. Trust issues can have an effect on the entire team, even if only one individual loses trust in another. And poor communication, especially the misreading of e-mail, makes trusting even more difficult.

Simply put, people who trust each other work more effectively, and they are more inclined to openly communicate, collaborate freely, innovate, and accomplish results.

Engendering Trust

Ask yourself these four questions:

1. *Do I exhibit predictable behavior?* If you want others to depend on you, your behavior can't be confusing, indecisive, or inconsistent. People need to make reasonable judgments about how you might react under new or different circumstances, and in order to do that you need to behave in a somewhat predictable manner. This consistency means, for example, that you will meet an agreed-upon protocol for informing others about key milestones.

2. *Do I follow through on my commitments?* People tend to treat you the way they have been treated by you. If you take your commitments seriously, others will, too.

3. *Do I communicate clearly or carelessly?* Miscommunications, especially in a virtual environment, add an extra hazard to trustworthiness. If you are clear about what you mean there is less chance that others will find your statements misleading.

4. *Am I honest or dishonest?* If you are knowingly careless with the truth, such as insisting that you never promised to call or e-mail at a specific time, then other people have good reason not to trust you. There is no such thing as a little bit of dishonesty.

Ten Rules for Building Trust in Your Virtual Team

Trust in virtual teams tends to be established—or not—right at the onset. It is during those first interactions, first stages, and first promises that Instant Trust occurs. After that, it evolves slowly through performance and consistency over time to become Lasting Trust.

Rule 1: Communicate, Communicate, Communicate!

Don't make remote teammates guess what you are thinking. Tell them. Unfortunately, remote teams and virtual teammates tend to believe that no news is bad news. A lack of interaction across distance erodes trust.

Make sure to use communication methods that simulate a face-to-face or one-on-one interaction as much as possible. Use pictures and voice along with data. Use Internet phone with video, or use computer technology to embed pictures on the intranet so that members can "see" each other online to help create social bonding and build trust.

Suggestions

➤ As the virtual team leader, define what ownership is and who is responsible for what pieces.

➤ Require each team member to communicate ideas and solutions for problems that arise.

➤ Make sure other teammates know that they are being listened to and convey that you are paying attention.

➤ Do not blame technology for communication failures—virtual teams are about people and relationships, not technology.

➤ You can't overcommunicate, so always increase communication and be prepared to listen.

Rule 2: Give Trust to Get Trust

The best way to create an environment of trust is to begin by trusting others. As a leader, you must set the example. Waiting to give trust to employees until they earn it is never as effective as assuming they are trustworthy unless they prove otherwise. As team members come to feel that you trust them, they will find it easier to trust you.

Suggestions

➤ Consider trust as an exchange that starts with giving. Once your trustworthiness influences others' trust in you, they will give you their trust in return. It is about reciprocity.

➤ Treat employees and colleagues with respect, even when they are impolite to you.

➤ Be prepared to give people the opportunity to demonstrate that they can be trusted.

➤ Take responsibility for your actions and give others the benefit of the doubt.

> Give recognition when it's deserved—don't try to take credit for the work of others.

> Promote your team to others; do not simply promote yourself.

Rule 3: Be Open and Honest

Honesty is the most important element of human trust. People respond to sincerity, self-disclosure, and openness. Share the good and bad news openly and provide information about your vision and actions. Hold honest conversations about what is going on, what you know, and what is on the horizon. Include your team members in these conversations and ask for their input. When you make a mistake, admit it and move on. Don't cover it up and ignore the consequences. Great leaders know that creating a climate that encourages open, honest conversation reduces politics, eliminates mistakes, and improves morale.

Suggestions

> Tell the truth.

> Keep staff members truthfully informed. Provide as much information as you can comfortably divulge as soon as possible in any situation.

> Display competence in supervisory and other work tasks. Know what you are talking about, and if you don't know, admit it.

> Give honest, just-in-time feedback to the person who is not performing.

> Mistakes will occur: Acknowledge what happened, talk through it, and learn from it.

> Be sincere and communicate with your team members on a regular basis to increase trust.

Rule 4: Keep Your Commitments

Again, this sounds like a cliché, and it is, but an important one at that. It's one of the golden rules and will go a long way toward building a productive relationship: *Do what you say and say what you will do—and make your actions noticeable.* Keep your promises and help people see the bigger picture. When leaders don't make their actions visible, it creates the perception that they don't follow through. This perception only increases when you factor in the physical distance between coworkers.

Suggestions

> ➤ Be reliable in keeping your promises.

> ➤ Act with integrity and keep commitments. If you cannot keep a commitment, explain what is happening in the situation without delay. Current behavior and actions are perceived by employees as the basis for predicting future behavior. Managers who act as if they are worthy of trust will more likely be followed with fewer complaints.

> ➤ Don't be late for conference calls or meetings.

> ➤ Don't hesitate, however, to speak to people who don't keep their promises.

Rule 5: Be Consistent

Trust results from consistent and predictable interaction over time. The process of building trust is not an event—it is a process. People tend to trust those who behave in a consistent manner, even if they do not like the actions. It provides a measure of comfort to know that we can count on someone to act in predictable ways. As is commonly said, "The devil you know is better than the devil you don't know."

Suggestions

> ➤ Treat all team members in a fair and consistent manner. Some remote team members may feel that they are being treated differently if there is an audio conference call from an office where other, "on-site" members are physically present. To ensure consistency, some managers use web conferencing with everyone at his own computer, even when some people are located on site.

> ➤ Be consistent because it demonstrates that you are stable and can be trusted.

> ➤ Act in a consistent manner with your employees because it will make them more engaged and involved in the interaction. As their comfort level increases, some people may take more risks.

> ➤ Stay positive even when things go wrong or you are faced with criticism.

Rule 6: Be Accessible and Responsive

Find ways to be regularly available to the team, even when involved in projects that take up your time and energy. Be sure to set regular virtual meeting times (via teleconference or videoconference), even when your team members work across multiple time zones. Let team members know that they will have an opportunity to address their questions or problems without a long waiting period.

Make sure to provide opportunities for interaction (planned or unplanned) because when the leader doesn't respond, or appears unresponsive, distrust is not far behind. Be action oriented. Avoid saying, "Let's think about it." Instead, say, "Let's do this or that." And then *do it!* Say what you mean, mean what you say, and follow through with actions. That will build your reputation for trustworthiness.

Suggestions

> ➤ Create a plan that lets everyone know when communication will and can take place. Include all the scheduled meetings and times you would normally be available to talk.

> ➤ Anticipate problems and be proactive.

> ➤ Be ready to give help when needed.

> ➤ Stay responsive—if you are being asked, respond.

Rule 7: Establish Agreements Up Front

Let your team know how and when you will respond to them. Then, honor those agreements throughout the life of the project or relationship. For example, a helpful protocol is to tell your virtual members that when they contact you, you pledge to respond within twenty-four

hours—unless it is an emergency, in which case you'll respond immediately. In general, establish time lines and deadlines, and provide answers, information, and the necessary data to move on. Lack of timely
response can look like a lack of concern or incompetence to someone,
thousands of miles away, who's staring at a deadline.

Suggestions

> ➤ Help your team build a common language and reference points.

> ➤ Let others know when you are reachable. Give them a sense of
> how you prefer to be reached (e.g., e-mail first, telephone sec-
> ond, text third) and let them know the best times of the day to
> reach you. Some virtual managers create virtual office hours
> when they are available at their desk and people can "pop by,"
> so to speak, using an IM, text message, or web chat to simulate
> dropping by the office in person.

> ➤ If agreed-on standards or rules aren't working, then do some-
> thing about them. They may need adjusting.

Rule 8: Maintain Confidences

Team members need to be able to express concerns, identify problems, share sensitive information, and surface relevant issues. Getting
agreements early on as to how confidential or sensitive data will be
handled is important. Remember, different cultures handle privacy issues differently.

Suggestions

> ➤ Keep your word.

> ➤ Help your team build a common language and reference points.

> ➤ Create an environment where members feel comfortable shar-
> ing relevant information.

> ➤ Respect others and deal with conflicts you may have with a
> team member in private and not in public.

> ➤ If you suspect a colleague is not being honest or is withholding
> information, have a word with the person in private.

Rule 9: Watch Your Language

A leader can unintentionally erode trust in subtle ways. Be careful not to use words that someone could construe as insulting. Don't refer to team members in remote locations as "them" or "those people." Don't use home office or cultural slang that may not transfer beyond your own country. Doing so will only widen the gap and increase someone's sense of isolation. It's a good idea to often check for understanding during a video or teleconference, and ask the speaker to clarify the meaning for others, if necessary. Or when e-mails contain jargon or acronyms that are unique to a function, location, or culture, follow up with clarification and then coach team members to avoid using such terms in future communications. In addition, avoid what could be perceived as vulgarity or profanity. It is best to stick with common professional business language, especially when working across organizational or ethnic cultures.

Suggestions

➤ Be a good example for people to follow. Remember, people look up to you and are observing your actions (and nonactions) particularly in the virtual environment, where trust is more fragile.

➤ Stay calm at times of difficulty or crisis.

➤ Protect the interest of all employees in a work group. Do not talk about absent employees or allow others to place blame, call names, or point fingers.

➤ Be aware of how you come across on the phone (e.g., communication style, how fast you talk, use of lingo/local slang words).

➤ Words are power—use them wisely.

Rule 10: Create Social Time for the Team

With on-site teams, much of the trust and confidence that team members have in one another and in the leader comes from informal social interaction. For virtual teams to have this experience requires a little more thought and creativity. It's a good idea to build informal socializing time into video or telephone conferences. At either the beginning or the end of a call, lead the way with informal conversation, such as asking about team members' outside interests or families. Begin by sharing something of your own, to break the ice.

Suggestions

> ➤ In the early stages of virtual team development, put your efforts into getting to know each other socially, rather than focusing totally on work.

> ➤ Create opportunities for team members to interact virtually.

> ➤ Make time for team members to play an online game together.

> ➤ Share international holidays with the team and discuss various customs/traditions.

Above all, trust comes from what you do over a period of time—the actions you take—and not from just saying the right words. Lasting Trust takes a long time to develop and can be lost in a moment. Do not take trust for granted.

> "Without trust, there cannot be cooperation between people, teams, departments, divisions. Without trust, each component will protect its own immediate interests to its own long-term detriment, and to the detriment of the entire system."
>
> —W. EDWARDS DEMING, FOUNDER OF THE QUALITY MOVEMENT

Creating Trust Synchronization

Even if your virtual team met once or twice in person, when a team is geographically dispersed, building and maintaining trust adds another dimension to an already-demanding process. And once you add the cross-cultural layer, trust can be your biggest challenge.

As a virtual manager, you must create what I call Trust Synchronization. Although we don't put a name to the day-to-day behaviors and thought processes that engender trust in a global workplace, we engage in an unspoken contract with each other to take the necessary steps to deliver organizational objectives. At the core of these behaviors and thought processes is the *expectation* that we can rely on another individual or group in a number of ways. That is what I mean by Trust Synchronization, and it involves four key principles:

➤ To be *honest*—Can I trust you to tell me the truth and say what's on your mind? (For example, will you admit a mistake, or give me constructive feedback?)

➤ To be *competent*—Can I trust that you are a capable member of the team, delivering high-quality work product? (For example, is your solution to a complex design issue accurate, pragmatic, and cost-effective?)

➤ To meet *commitments*—Can I trust that you will do what you said you would do? (For example, will you meet an agreed-upon deadline and keep me in the loop, as promised, if I am not present at a meeting?)

➤ To *represent* me although I am not in the room—Can I trust that you will consider my interests even though we work in physically dispersed locations, with diminished cues to communicate sensitive business and people issues? (For example, will you include my team's expertise when deciding on who will work on project X?)

Let's take a closer look at each of these four principles of Trust Synchronization.

Honesty-Trust Definition

There is nothing more important in trust than the simple fact of just telling the truth. That is the basis of Honesty-Trust, and that's why it is the first element of creating Trust Synchronization.

Trust occurs when I trust you to tell me what is really happening. It has to do with integrity. This is true whether team members are colocated or disbursed, but in the virtual environment it becomes especially critical because I cannot see you and need to depend on your word. Being honest and thinking that others are honest is the strongest predictor of trust. And to assess Honesty-Trust, one can look at how consistently people met their obligations in the past, aligning them with original goals and results. Therefore, Honesty-Trust has to do with telling the truth and fulfilling one's commitments.

Honesty-Trust Behaviors

➤ Tell the truth.

➤ Share all available information.

➤ Raise issues that you have early on.

> ➤ Raise concerns as they arise.

> ➤ Stand up for your team members.

> ➤ Deliver on what you say you will do.

> ➤ Ask advice from others because it shows that you are open to suggestions.

> ➤ Consider and discuss both sides of an issue, good and bad.

Competence-Trust Definition

Competence-Trust has to do with someone's ability to do the job, with the skills, knowledge, and behaviors that build competence. It also has to do with team members' perceptions of one another's skill practices, content qualifications, and organizational perspective. If people perceive you as providing good-quality work and contributing relevant, interesting ideas, you will gain credibility as a competent individual. Therefore, Competence-Trust involves the skills and behaviors that help people learn, perform job responsibilities, and influence outcomes.

Competence-Trust Behaviors

> ➤ Manage time and priorities well.

> ➤ Do your homework and background research.

> ➤ Make good decisions.

> ➤ Take initiatives.

> ➤ Demonstrate motivation.

> ➤ Actively seek out information.

Commitment-Trust Definition

Are you going to follow through on what you said you will do? Can I trust you to meet your deadlines and keep me in the loop? In the virtual environment, the most significant way to demonstrate that you are committed is to produce results. Team members cannot see that you are staying late to finish the deliverable or that you are working through the weekend. They can only see your results and whether you got things done on time, within budget, and within the protocols set up front for your assignment. Commitment-Trust also involves response time and completing tasks within appropriate time frames. In fact, I once observed a situation where two team members were fully committed to getting the job done, but since they worked virtually on two different technology platforms, they did not complete tasks on time and lost Commitment-Trust in their organization.

Commitment-Trust Behaviors

- ➤ Think ahead.
- ➤ Do what you say you will do.
- ➤ Follow through on deadlines.
- ➤ Respond to e-mails even after business hours.
- ➤ Help other team members.
- ➤ Do tasks that are not required of you.
- ➤ Conduct research for an upcoming project before it has officially started.
- ➤ Write down all of your project deadlines and post them in a place where everyone on your team can see them.

Representation-Trust Definition

Representation-Trust is the principle that has impacted me more than the other three, probably because I had an "aha!" moment several years ago when working with a virtual team that was struggling with trust-building expectations. The team members were stuck on ways they could implement Honesty-Trust, Competence-Trust, and Commitment-Trust behaviors. After several sessions we kept discussing the three elements, but they did not understand their connection to establishing trust with other team members who were located elsewhere. How was this different from on-site teams?

Then I had a sudden insight—in the virtual environment the trust differentiator is that the other person *is not in the room*. So how do you trust someone you cannot see? What do you do when the person representing you resides in another part of the country or the world? I realized that a fourth type of trust existed, which I call Representation-Trust, and it rounds out the Wheel of Trust™ model (shown in Figure 4-3 and as detailed in the next section). By definition, this kind of trust is an identification-based trust since individuals cannot see each other but may "permit" another party to serve as their agent when not in the room. Similarly, we entrust lawyers and accountants to represent us in trials and audits. Representation-Trust has to do with the ways that *you* represent *me* and consider my interests, even though the virtual setting means we are subjected to diminished cues to communicate sensitive business and people issues.

Representation-Trust Behaviors

➤ My "representative" generally agrees with me about how work issues and deadlines are handled. We both have a similar work ethic and problem-solving style.

➤ Anyone who acts as a representative for me or others on the team must have a strong understanding of the company, professional communication skills (oral and written), an amiable personality, a keen ability to build rapport quickly, good videoconferencing etiquette, and knowledge of other people's cultural values and culturally sensitive issues.

➤ To represent me or others on the team well, people who act as representatives have to be able to present themselves well.

Everything revolves around trust when you work with others. If you don't trust each other, you can't succeed together. For Lasting Trust to occur in the virtual environment, the four trust elements must work together to create Trust Synchronization. Some people refer to this outcome as credibility. Or, as a CEO of a construction company said, "There is trust because they just know you." I like to refer to it as the human connection in a virtual world.

The Wheel of Trust™

To the extent that virtual members honor these four elements, trust exists and accountability is achieved. If accountability is the gold standard, leading to business success, then teammates need to act in a credible manner. If we visualize these four elements as the spokes in a wheel (Figure 4-3), with accountability as the axle that holds them in place, one can see that when the spokes are not well aligned, the wheel cannot properly support the car's momentum, and the journey will be far from smooth.

Picture yourself as an executive driving down the global superhighway neck and neck with your competitors. To gain an edge, leaders require a cohesive and knowledgeable team, whose members support each other with accurate and timely information. On-site teams can provide this support; however, on the global superhighway, members are dispersed over wide distances, creating conditions that erode trust, such as the lack of face-to-face interaction, communication and cultural barriers, and workdays that span many time zones. These are challenging circumstances for virtual team leaders who strive to align the Wheel of Trust™.

Figure 4-3. Wheel of Trust™ (AIM Strategies®; Applied Innovative Management®).

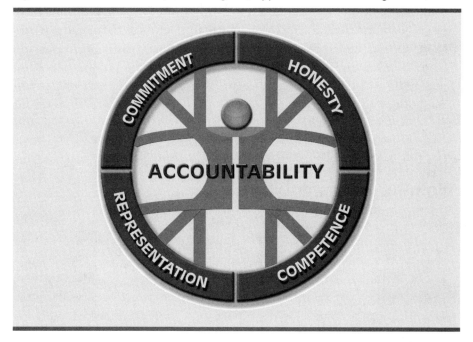

Your Wheel of Trust™

- Which element (spoke) presents the greatest challenge for you?
- What factors contribute to the difficulties this element presents to you?
- What type of issues do you face around this element?

Expectations and Reactions

- What expectations do you have for teammates regarding Honesty-Trust?
- What expectations do you identify with Competence-Trust?
- What expectations do you identify with Commitment-Trust?
- What expectations do you identify with Representation-Trust?

Virtual teams are encouraged to establish a few accountability agreements that support building or, if necessary, rebuilding a trusting team environment. This encourages teams to document the trust-building relationships that are most important to them and hold each other accountable. You can have your team members participate in this exercise together to remind them that building trust is an important step. Thank them for their willingness to keep the commitments they just made and encourage team members to support one another as they implement new behaviors.

Aligning the Wheel of Trust™: Attaining Accountability

Figure 4-4 outlines what you and your team members have to do to achieve clarity around trust. If you take these actions, you are well on the way to sharing accountability to attain common goals. Global leaders of virtual teams face the further challenge of establishing and maintaining solid connections without the support of physical cues and with less organizational support than their counterparts in colocated teams enjoy.

Figure 4-4. Wheel of Trust™: trust builders.

Element	Behaviors and Actions
Honesty	Align your words and actions: • Display the behaviors you want to promote within the team at virtual and in-person meetings. • Ask teammates for feedback on the consistency of your words and actions. • Take the time to explain to your team members if your actions are not consistent. Act with integrity: • Do the right thing in the best interest of the team's business goals. • Be able to say "I don't agree" to those above you. • To the best of your ability, have a team reward system in place that encourages cooperation and shared effort. • Speak up for your commitments with the team and with senior management. • In tough circumstances, continue to do the right thing, even in a crisis or "firefighting" situation.
Commitment	Follow through on commitments and show results: • Publish a log of commitments and post them for all stakeholders to see. Have a method to ensure follow-through. • Keep promises even if circumstances have changed. • Keep your commitments in cost, schedule, and technical areas. Inform team members well in advance if you will be late in any area. • Stay knowledgeable about deadlines and work issues so that you can identify problems before you have to defend them.
Competence	Display competence: • Focus on individual and team results. • Keep current in your technical area of expertise and continue to refine your skills. • Be open to new ideas and methods. • Be able to say "I don't know." • Allow others to be experts. • Foster expertise and sharing on the team.
Representation	Consider teammates who are not physically present: • Help new members ramp up as quickly as possible. • Circulate biographical information when new members join the team. • When possible, hold a face-to-face meeting. If that is not possible, do the next best thing with the technology available to the entire team. • Build your relationship with team members in other locations so that you develop an understanding of their point of view. • Contact team members about problems before commenting to others about possible reasons for them. • Don't speak negatively about a virtual teammate's decisions without going on record and telling the person of your intentions to do so.

(continued)

Figure 4-4. (continued)

- Post information and decisions so that all stakeholders have full access.
- Ensure that everyone receives information in a timely manner. Use multiple, synchronous, asynchronous, and redundant communication methods.
- Show all sides of an issue, and create a mechanism to air disagreements and to discuss and debate issues.
- Have standard processes for selecting team members, rewarding people, assigning tasks, and sharing information, and make sure these processes don't favor certain cultures or locations.
- Rotate the "good" and "bad" team jobs.
- Help members to transition off the team and to new assignments.

What Does Accountability Look Like?

At the onset of the chapter, we learned that accountability in the virtual world is about clarity, operations rhythm, and performance. But mostly it is about you. An individual who *behaves* in an accountable manner:

➤ *Acts in Predictable Ways and Is Dependable.* Behaving predictably creates parameters within which team members can operate without continually checking back for further information or instruction. Inconsistent behavior makes it hard for people to know what they can expect or where to place their trust. (Of course, sometimes leaders shift direction based on changes in business conditions that render past actions obsolete.) Behavior, however, is based on values and principles that guide one's actions. This is especially true when the individuals who are affected by your actions are many miles away and lack context and supporting cues to fully understand the situation.

➤ *Manages Team Members' Expectations.* How we manage another person's expectations of us goes a long way to determining accountability. Sometimes expectations are not met because they have not been identified or understood—a situation easy to picture in a virtual environment. Clarity is key, because without it intentions are misconstrued and perceptions become mismatched. When someone's expectations are not met the person can feel disappointed, frustrated, or worse. Often, the result is a lack of trust, which prevents accountability.

Some expectations are explicitly conveyed, while others are merely implied. To succeed, global leaders need to manage relationships throughout the organization and think through the various written and unwritten "contracts" they have.

Explicit expectations are clearly stated and understood by all parties. When people act within these parameters, trust forms and people can work effectively, even when they do not share the same physical location yet bear joint responsibility for work product.

Implicit expectations arise from agreements or mutual understandings that are unwritten or unspoken. In a virtual environment they can occur frequently, since time constraints prevent continually checking and fine-tuning every detail. Unfortunately, sometimes a negative impact from unwritten agreements is not noticed until something has dropped through the cracks. A rule of thumb: If you work closely with someone and share similar beliefs, work style, and worldview, your implicit expectations have a greater chance of being met. The opposite is true when you merely assume that a team member from a different culture, where communication barriers may exist, shares your understanding.

➤ *Accepts Responsibility for Deliverables.* President Harry Truman was legendary for having a sign on his desk that read, THE BUCK STOPS HERE. Few qualities engender accountability more than simply acknowledging your part in a written or unwritten contract without assigning responsibility elsewhere. Busy executives, with large spans of control, are unable to control every variable. Mistakes are made on their watch. However, a good faith attempt to admit them openly and work to correct them can go a long way to making you credible.

➤ *Confronts Obstacles.* Hand in hand with accepting responsibility is confronting obstacles with the intention of removing them—without spending time and energy blaming people or processes for their existence. The nature of business is fixing problems, or creating new problems, which then require fixing! In a virtual environment, where it is often difficult to get your hands around the actual obstacle, you can be a "blocker" or "fixer" of problems. Those who actively tackle issues in order to move business goals forward quickly develop a reputation as accountable team members.

➤ *Follows Through on Commitments.* People can depend on you to follow through on your commitments. When you keep agreements with others, you empower the relationship and build trust. Obviously, when someone repeatedly breaks agreements, trust is compromised and the relationship disintegrates. In a virtual environment, where time constraints prevent continual interchange among stakeholders, it is impossible to share every decision. Therefore, great care should be taken to promise what is doable. Global leaders get into trouble when they overpromise for expediency's sake and yet fall short on deliverables. Unfortunately, people tend to remember the promises you didn't keep far longer than the promises you kept.

It seems obvious that (1) leaders earn trust not by words but by deeds, and (2) leaders lose trust when they don't act consistently or fail to follow through on commitments.

➤ *Respects Team Members and Provides Support as Needed.* If you respect your team members' skills, abilities, and judgment, then you are willing to rely on them for key deliverables, and you treat them as partners in accomplishing goals. In a virtual environment, you often have to take a leap of faith in trusting someone you don't know well, who may not even speak your language fluently, to handle a complex, technical issue. However, micromanaging is not a viable option for global leaders in the twenty-first century. A wiser strategy is to have in place support systems that recognize and encourage competence and open communication.

YOUR VIRTUAL ROADMAP TO TRUST AND ACCOUNTABILITY

Behaviors Identified with Accountability	I Do Well	I Could Do Better
• Act in predictable ways so that others can depend on you.		
• Manage team members' expectations.		
• Accept responsibility for deliverables within your span of control.		
• Confront obstacles.		
• Follow through on commitments.		
• Respect team members and provide support as needed.		

Accountability Action Plan

Component	Behaviors and Actions I Am Committing to	Time Frame
Act in predictable ways		
Manage expectations		
Accept responsibility for deliverables		
Confront obstacles		
Follow through on commitments		
Respect team members and provide support		

CHAPTER **5**

Defusing Conflict and Overcoming Roadblocks

W hy is the potential for conflict in the virtual world so great? The lack of structure compared with the traditional workplace creates many more opportunities for misunderstandings, inconsistencies, communication barriers, and ways to fly under the radar. Managerial oversight is spread thin, and members from different cultures who may speak other languages work in complex situations. Unfortunately, the conditions for conflict to arise appear all too easily.

Here's what your peers say about conflict in the virtual world:

> "The main source of virtual conflict occurs when people don't have the same expectations about outcomes or goals. Confusion occurs around who is doing what, who is allocated how many hours, and personality differences."
>
> —VIRTUAL LEADER, INVESTOR RELATIONS

> "The biggest virtual conflict involves communication or lack thereof: How come I wasn't told? How come no one communicated with me? Other conflicts between virtual team members happen when people don't pull their weight. Generally, they don't talk to each other. They go to the project manager, and the project manager has to deal with it."
>
> —PROJECT MANAGER, PHARMACEUTICAL COMPANY

> "Since you don't have body language and eye contact, which are so much a part of how we communicate, verbal or e-mail messages can be easily misinterpreted. There are many more misunderstandings in the virtual environment. For example, e-mail blasts across the organization can be more risky than yelling down the hallway. Conflict can arise from misinterpreting an e-mail sent out of emotion or not fully thought through."
>
> —FIELD OPERATIONS MANAGER, GOURMET FOOD COMPANY

Are these situations familiar to you? Conflict happens. Regardless of work arrangements, confusion and obstacles are bound to occur. However, by its nature, the virtual environment lends itself more easily to situational conflicts than traditional work arrangements. When colleagues aren't in close contact they can "hide," and so conflicts may be overlooked or may lie under the surface for a long period of time before problems are noticed. As a virtual leader, you want to be a little more vigilant about detecting the early warning signs that friction is bubbling up or that a breakdown in communication is imminent.

Conflicts, even minor ones, need to be addressed early or they tend to spiral out of control, especially in the virtual environment. For example, conflicts can arise from simple e-mail miscommunications that turn into challenging situations. In essence, the potential for conflict exists whenever people perceive a concern or preference differently, and each person champions his or her own position.

There are four typical types of virtual conflicts: performance conflict, identity conflict, data conflict, and social conflict.

Performance Conflict: What Am I Supposed to Do and How Should I Do It?

There are many instances in the virtual world that lend themselves to performance conflict. Reasonable people may differ about work-related issues: What tasks need to be performed—and how should they be carried out? What resources are needed to move a project forward? Who needs what from a colleague or team? How do we clarify processes and procedures for those who need to know, but whose language skills make communication difficult? What is the best way to solve problem X? Although unresolved conflicts may lead to lower performance, some conflict can energize performance and actually increase team success (achievement), especially if the issue is quickly resolved.

> "There is always some virtual conflict about performance. The greatest conflict comes out of not having a clearly defined mission or purpose, [with] no way to measure the group's performance or to hold people accountable. And if the manager doesn't have a strong statement about what the team is set up to do—no clearly defined objectives/deliverables—that's where conflicts lie."
>
> —VT LEADER, MEDICAL DEVICES

> "The main source of conflict on my teams is the different perspectives and differences in priorities. It occurs all the time, every day. I have 100 people, each wanting something right away. Because they are not aware of each other's needs and they can't be told for reasons of confidentiality, it's very hard. I have to share resources, share ideas, share lessons learned from one country's program with another, but it's tough to set priorities, respond quickly, and perform. It's a lot of pressure."
>
> —VIRTUAL MANAGER, NGO HUMANITARIAN RELIEF

Identity Conflict: Where Do I Belong?

Virtual team members are often placed in situations in which they report to multiple managers in matrixed organizations. Tension and confusion regarding priorities occur when colleagues switch back and forth between assignments. Many people serve on several project teams simultaneously and may have an identity crisis when they must switch between multiple priorities and projects. Often, virtual members are committed to multiple projects and simultaneously report to both a local on-site manager and a virtual manager, making it difficult to figure out priorities.

> "Many people have dual accountability to their local manager and their functional manager and struggle with ways to handle two bosses who may not be in agreement regarding results. The problem isn't that multiple managers ask the team member to do too many things; it's that they ask [the team member] to do so many things at the same time. You have to make sure that work efforts aren't duplicated."
>
> —VT LEADER, PHARMACEUTICAL FIRM

> "Given that virtual teams have many skill sets, you need roles defined for them. In the United States, we defined three roles—team lead, database administrator, and communication specialist—and we understood that this arrangement was based on American experience. We ran into situations where the team in India redefined the role for database administrator—theirs served different projects while ours served one client. Their understanding was, 'I have fifteen hours/week dedicated to project X and then I focus on other ones.' So we ran into identity crises problems."
>
> —MANAGER, TELECOM COMPANY

Data Conflict: What Should I Focus on First?

Since virtual teams rely on technology as a communications vehicle more than their traditional counterparts do, there is a greater potential for information overload with the sheer volume of simultaneous communication that can bombard team members. Conflict occurs because individuals cannot handle so much data at once; they may unintentionally forget or miss important details. Not only does information overload cause stress, but the potential to lose track of certain important details can cause conflict if it results in certain tasks being neglected.

> "The biggest problem with getting too much information and, in particular, using e-mails is that they can easily become overwhelming. Although you can set some standards about writing, proofreading, and sending e-mails, it's easy to go overboard and hit 'reply all' or 'cc:' everyone. I get over 1,000 e-mails a day, and I must go through them [all] or risk missing important information."
>
> —VT LEADER, COMPUTER SOFTWARE COMPANY

Not long ago I had the following experience with a coaching engagement for a senior executive at a financial services firm: After several preliminary meetings, we set a time to begin the sessions right after the executive's planned and much-needed vacation. We met the afternoon of his return, and when I walked into his office he immediately pointed out that his in-box had more than 10,000 messages (apparently, he vacationed at a remote location with limited e-mail access), so there was no way he could take time for our session. The memory is still vivid. When he tried to explain why he wouldn't, or couldn't, concentrate on the coaching session, he started crying, literally crying. "How can I get through this mountain of data?" he said. "What should I focus on first? It will take me days to sort through this information and I have meetings to attend and work to do. Even if I work at night, it will take time from my family and personal life."

Clearly, his emotional state precluded a typical coaching session about leadership style, team dynamics, and other issues that we agreed to address. Instead, we sat at his computer and I helped sort through his in-box. For two hours we looked at messages. E-mails that did not require a response were deleted, simple requests were addressed, and short e-mails were sent to colleagues who wanted updates to explain that they would be forthcoming as soon as possible. We also came up with a better system for incoming e-mails, including organizing messages by subject lines and creating subfolders for lower-priority items.

Here, then, was an example of data conflict. Despite the fact that technology is an essential tool in modern business, it also creates situations where any one of us can swim in a sea of data overload.

Social Conflict: Who Are the People on My Team and What Are Their Personalities?

Social conflict can be defined as personality clashes or the tensions that arise between people because of differing interpersonal styles. Social conflict often arises on a virtual team because members do not have the time or opportunity to create strong relationships with teammates, which tend to minimize the impact of misunderstandings. The flexibility inherent in face-to-face contact, with direct (verbal) and nonverbal communication cues, is missing here, and so an opportunity to understand why people act a certain way is lost.

Instead of giving someone else the benefit of the doubt, we may retreat deeper into our own point of view, because it is easier to ignore or circumvent unpleasant situations. Even if we choose to ignore the conflict ("He's so far away, I really don't have to deal with him most of the time"), we tend to harp on negative feelings. Conflict can surface and lead to intense exchanges, but more commonly it is ignored until a flash point causes an explosion. In any case, work product is affected, with potential negative consequences down the road.

> "Personality conflicts between people via e-mail can affect the entire team. This happened on my team between two people who were on different continents and interpreted e-mail differently. It was exhausting because they jumped on every word and it became worse because of their philosophical difference. It became a 'flaming e-mail' that went back and forth for weeks. Each person misunderstood and misinterpreted the written word. I finally had to jump in and conduct a mediation call."
> —SOFTWARE IPO STRATEGY OFFICER

> "When there is no sense of an intact project team or any team camaraderie, it can create a lack of empathy on the virtual team. This sounds touchy-feely, but it's about being unable to take the other person's perspective, see their point of view, or even understand why they do what they do, because the social element is missing."
> —CONSULTANT, INTERNATIONAL REDEVELOPMENT ORGANIZATION

What Type of Conflict Is It?

A problem that occurs in all teams, and especially in virtual teams, is that members often do not really know the form of conflict with which they are dealing. What may appear to be social conflict is really performance conflict. To clarify misunderstandings early on, you need to be aware of differences and how to overcome conflict roadblocks. Team members need time together and the experience of communicating with each other to develop trust, so they can open up and speak about difficult issues. If not, misunderstandings are more likely to end in conflict about inconsistencies, mismatched wishes, or conflicting desires and disagreements.

Adding the Cultural Factor

Cross-cultural workplace conflicts resemble car crashes. Sometimes they are minor events involving a couple of cars, and sometimes the damage is greater. Conflict situations are hard for all of us. But in the daily rush hours of our lives, when we add cultural differences to the constant traffic of heavy workloads, multiple deadlines, and occasional roadblocks, "crashes" are inevitable.

What happens when employees from different cultures react to conflict situations differently? How do these situations get resolved so that goals are accomplished and long-term working relationships are not negatively impacted?

Several virtual managers I spoke with said that the biggest source of conflict in the virtual environment centered on understanding the meaning of certain phrases. They refer to this type of conflict as "overcoming differences." In other words, they would walk people through examples, give specific instructions, and still certain phrases were misinterpreted. One virtual leader from a major insurance company described a situation: "I had a half-hour phone conversation with English-speaking colleagues from Asia, but I couldn't understand them and their accent," he told me. "The technology we used made it hard to hear [each other]. People weren't always saying the same thing in the same way, so I always had to clarify: 'John, did you say A, B, and C?' He would answer, 'No, no, B, C, and D.' I then followed up: 'So, you said B, C, and D?' Finally he said, 'No, no, B, D, and F.' That's how I learned to overcome our differences and communicate."

In addition to language barriers, different cultures handle conflicts in their own way. For example, Asians place a high priority on saving face. Americans value direct communication and there is less reliance on nonverbal behavior. When team members are from different cultures, there is, then, a potential for greater conflict, and managers need to know how to handle the situation. These cross-cultural factors/elements are explored further in Chapter 7, but for now this chapter focuses on overcoming obstacles in the virtual environment, regardless of whatever cultural misunderstandings might occur. Figure 5-1 summarizes the main conflict types and how to recognize them.

Figure 5-1. Questions to consider concerning conflict types.

Conflict Type	Conflict Occurrence	Questions to Ask Yourself
Performance Conflict *What am I to do and how should I do it?*	• Team destination was not reinforced early on. • Project is not clear and responsibilities are not well defined. • Ambiguity exists about how to do the task or how to delegate resources.	• In conflict situations, do you tend to forget what you initially wanted? • Do you discontinue a project because you become unclear about what you are doing and why? • Are you unable to begin a project because you are unsure of first steps?
Identity Conflict *Where do I belong?*	• There are different perspectives around various priorities. • Managers do not stay on top of schedules, resource allocation, and clear priorities.	• Are you unable to meet all the deadlines from your multiple bosses? • Have you asked your managers to help you handle multiple priorities? • Did you ask for specific deadline dates?
Data Conflict *What should I focus on first?*	• You receive a great deal of information—some of it may be duplicated. • Information comes from multiple sources without a flag indicating which is urgent. • Information is not updated at the same time and in the same way.	• Do you receive too many e-mails after being away for only a few hours? • Do you often receive e-mails that repeat information—and are still unsure if they can be deleted?
Social Conflict *Who are the people on my team and what are their personalities?*	• The people on your team don't know each other well. • The Team Setup phase was overlooked. • Team members have not had face-to-face time. • Personalities differ.	• Do you find yourself debating or arguing when you are in a conflict situation? • Do you "stand your ground"— that is, you won't be easily persuaded during conflict situations?

Reacting to Conflict

During many workshop presentations I have given over the years, I would post a picture of a man and a woman seated at a table, facing each other, right hands clasped in an arm-wrestling posture. Then I would ask participants, "What is your reaction to this picture? Is it good or bad conflict?" Invariably I would get a mixed reaction. Some participants viewed conflict in a positive light because they saw two individuals playfully engaged in a tug-of-war, while others viewed it more negatively, seeing a struggle. These common reactions are outlined in Figure 5-2. The point I made was that conflict is not good or bad; it's how you approach it that matters.

Then I would explore the real question: Why is it important to deal with and manage conflict?

Differences in opinions are common among teammates, friends, family members, organizations, and people, in general. Some level of disagreement is healthy because it can generate ideas and build innovation. When everyone always agrees, it is difficult to come up with creative solutions. Many times conflicts result from simple mismatches in perception. These misunderstandings can contribute to more serious

Figure 5-2. Common reactions to conflict situations.

What is your reaction to conflict? Is it good or bad conflict?	
Possible Reactions: Good	**Possible Reactions: Bad**
• Normal and natural interpersonal dynamics	• Negative, destructive interactions
• Can lead to creative, improved results or solutions	• Shows someone can't get along with others/not a team player
• Challenges the status quo/complacent thinking	• Inhibits progress/getting things done
	• Creates chaos and confusion
Keywords Associated with "Good" Conflict: *multiple choice, discovery, bridge, fireworks, sunrise, renewed energy*	Keywords Associated with "Bad" Conflict: *wrestling, explosion, collision, headache, rejection, struggle, battle, tug-of-war*

conflict issues around speed, results, or personalities, and they may have reverberations that are felt beyond the immediate department or work unit. When stress levels are high (as they often are in the virtual environment), conflicts are more likely to arise. Sudden changes in organizational policy or company direction can cause confusion and lead to conflict. A quick e-mail can spark conflict, as can a casual comment or suggestion during a telephone conference. Virtual team members often feel indifferent toward each other unless they previously took the time to explore commonalities, beginning the process of team bonding. That is why I highly recommend conducting a Team Setup session early in the team's life cycle. Often the common bonds formed in those early days help to defuse conflict situations later on.

Common reactions to conflict include feelings of betrayal and missed expectations or a simple avoidance of dealing with the issue—any of which may lead to decreased productivity. Virtual employees might avoid a conflict because they do not know how to constructively handle it or they may be afraid of what confronting conflict would do to their reputation. While conflict avoidance seems the easier choice, I've seen many negative consequences in the long term when that happens. Sometimes employees become disengaged and don't speak up, or they wait until things escalate to the boiling point. Subtle examples of conflict avoidance include hitting the mute button and multitasking while on a conference call; not paying attention when a question is asked; and, finally, total disengagement. These actions often result in loss of work quality and indifference; however, the greatest cost is the human cost. Morale and energy suffer because employees are angry and frustrated. Some people may internalize what they hear and start backbiting or plotting to "one-up" another person. What started as a molehill can become an overwhelming mountain.

How can you prevent paying the huge price of conflict and instead reap the benefits of a productive work environment in which teammates work effectively with each other? The first step is to lower barriers to communication and motivation by learning how to handle conflict reactions and turn conflicts into problem-solving opportunities. This chapter includes several tips for resolving conflicts, particularly those common to the virtual environment. First, though, let's focus on the productive and destructive dimensions of conflict, levels of conflict, aspects of conflict, and explore a real-life case study that combines all these elements.

Dimensions of Conflict

Although the word *conflict* tends to connote something negative, it does not necessarily have to be destructive. Conflict situations, when appropriately handled, can yield productive results. If virtual teammates can recognize and defuse potential conflict situations before harm is caused, they provide growth opportunities. Figure 5-3 gives examples of the productive and destructive characteristics of conflict.

Figure 5-3. Productive and destructive characteristics of conflict.

PRODUCTIVE	DESTRUCTIVE
Opens up issues of importance so that they can be clarified	Diverts energy from more important activities and issues
Results in solutions to problems	Deepens differences in values
Increases team members' involvement in issues that affect them	Polarizes groups so that internal rigidity develops among some team members, reducing intergroup cooperation
Helps teammates grow personally and apply what they learn to future situations	Produces irresponsible and inflammatory behavior (name-calling, fights, e-mail bashing)
Helps build cohesiveness among team members as they share and learn about each other	Destroys the morale of team members or reinforces poor self-images
Serves as a release for hidden emotions and anxiety	Produces anger and heightened emotions that may cause people to shut down
Leads to authentic communication	Creates a barrier to communication and impairs relationships

Levels of Conflict

According to Richard De George's Ethical Displacement Theory, there are three levels to conflict: interpersonal, organizational, and societal/cultural.*

Level	Examples
Interpersonal	Conflict with family, friends, neighbors, and relationships at work; may include personality clashes, misunderstandings with colleagues, and personal problems
Organizational	Conflict with corporate policy changes, mergers, client issues, vendor problems, other teams, and business associations
Societal	Conflict dealing with the environment, cross-cultural differences, country regulations, and society (the world) as a whole

Some conflict dilemmas must be resolved at a level other than the level at which they are manifested. For example, an interpersonal conflict between an employee and his or her manager (e.g., a disagreement over a performance appraisal) may need to be handled at the organizational level (in this case by company policy) or across physical boundaries.

---

*De George, Richard, *Business Ethics,* 7th ed. (Englewood Cliffs, NJ: Prentice Hall, 2009).

Aspects of Conflict

During team events or workshops that focus on team building, I often draw a triangle (as shown in Figure 5-4) to explain three aspects of conflict that I call the Who, How, and What or the three Ps: People, Process, and Problem. They reside at the root cause of any conflict situation.

Figure 5-4. Three Ps of conflict resolution.

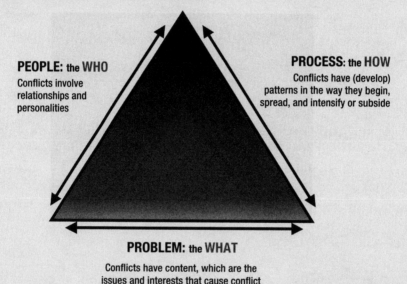

PEOPLE: the WHO
Conflicts involve relationships and personalities

PROCESS: the HOW
Conflicts have (develop) patterns in the way they begin, spread, and intensify or subside

PROBLEM: the WHAT
Conflicts have content, which are the issues and interests that cause conflict

The Who (People). Conflicts are about individuals, even though they sometimes involve collections of individuals where there are relationships and personalities, such as in organizations (e.g., the IT department, human resources, operations, sales) or cultures (e.g., the Chinese, Americans, Russians).

The How (Process). Conflicts always have causes and play out in recognizable patterns over time. You can identify historical patterns (e.g., "The IT department never responds quickly enough"). You can see what kinds of responses exist over time (e.g., "They have a tendency to keep it all in until they explode in anger").

The What (Problem). This is the source or issue at the heart of any conflict. It may be about self-respect, or inequality, or simple annoyance ("I don't like his mannerisms"). All conflicts, big or small, are about issues or interests.

Knowing clearly the Who, How, and What of a conflict situation is the first step to resolving it, and doing a little reflection can further help you handle conflicts. For instance, contemplate these questions:

1. What conditions may lead to conflict in your environment?

2. What are some of the consequences of not managing conflict?

3. What approaches or strategies do you currently use to deal with conflict?

Here's a quick scenario based on an actual conflict situation that I was called in to help resolve. After reading the case study, please reflect on how you would act in a similar situation. Later on in this chapter, I'll offer specific tips and steps for handling conflict and undertaking mediation.

CASE STUDY

Hurt Feelings Lead to Hurting the Business

William, the vice president of accounting for his division, works at corporate headquarters in London and has a dotted-line responsibility for a global accounting team that spans three other locations—Cape Town, Seoul, and Houston. He has committed this team to standardizing all financial reporting for the division because sales and marketing could no longer project inventory accurately using an "apples and oranges" approach to global customers. The target date for replacing the old system was the end of the current fiscal year, and until that time, all centers would have to run dual systems. Although the company was based in London (mainly because its founder was British), by far the largest operation was in Houston. Leo, Houston's top finance manager, previously spent more than a year in London working on a complex project. While on this assignment he formed tight bonds with many key managers and gained a comprehensive understanding of the business at the granular level. He assumed that he was next in line for the vice presidency. When William was selected, Leo either ignored him or communicated solely on a need-to-know basis.

The relationship never warmed, and unfortunately, the stakes kept getting higher. Starting with small differences on how to report data, the two men's disagreements spread to issues about revamping the larger, complex financial system. Leo believed (as did his day-to-day boss, Jack, the head of Houston's operation) that since Houston generated well over 50 percent of the profits for the division, any major, division-wide change should be approved by managers at that location. He directed his staff to continue to rely on the old system, did not devote adequate resources to test the new system, and communicated as little as possible with William. William found out indirectly that Leo was not supporting his efforts and set up a videoconference to discuss progress (or lack of) on testing the new system. Leo explained that he did not have sufficient staff to run parallel systems; the new system required more resources than were available. Then he exploded, letting loose these comments: "You picked this darn system because it's based in Liverpool, not because it was robust enough to handle the business, especially over here. If you want it tested, send some of your people here on assignment. I don't have the time, and neither do my people. If that's not good enough, deal with Jack." With that, Leo turned off the video and walked away.

Situations with similar issues and consequences to the one described occur far too frequently in business. What type of conflict is involved here? Standardizing financial reporting for the division across all locations was mandated, and parallel systems needed to be run. Performance conflict arose when William made testing the new system his priority, but Leo refused to commit the resources needed to run dual systems, to test the new one, and to meet the year-end deadline. More important, social conflict was involved as well. The root of this type of conflict is twofold: Leo resented William for getting a promotion he believed he deserved and did not cooperate with him from the beginning. William was not sensitive to Leo's resentment and ignored the fact that this key player's support was critical to his own success.

The situation could have been turned around with sensible, practical actions such as planning regular status meetings, during which the key players could have continually addressed deadline issues, and then putting in place relentless follow-up procedures. In addition, each team member should have had clear roles and responsibilities, with communication guidelines understood by all. Finally, accountability mechanisms needed to exist to build trust within the team. Both leaders made this situation worse by ignoring their differences, which were small at first, but grew to have larger implications for the entire division. Without communicating with each other their difficulties grew to the point that a key project was threatened. William should have understood earlier that Leo was not forthcoming or cooperative and tried to make him an ally through ongoing communications. Leo, as a key manager, should have seen the "larger picture" and put aside personal resentments to address business concerns. He could have asked William to work more closely with him to gain an understanding of what resources were available and how the finance area could best support the business, especially since Leo's location was the most profitable in the division.

The social conflict elements are more difficult to defuse because they often simmer below the surface, and in business situations people prefer to avoid touchy-feely behavior. However, when one person is promoted over another, it makes sense for the new leader to recognize that it is in everyone's best interests to reach out, build a bridge, and make the other party a partner. How to build that bridge depends on the flexibility of both individuals.

Resolution of the Conflict

What actually happened in this case? Text messages went flying across both sides of the Atlantic, and Jack quickly realized that this conflict would have a negative impact on the bottom line. At this point he called me in to help mediate the situation, which I diagnosed as involving both performance and social conflict.

To assess the situation I had individual videoconferences with Jack and Leo in Houston, and William in London. The facts I gleaned from these conversations were as follows: London HQ had committed to installing a new system; Leo was not committing the needed resources to test this system, with Jack's tacit approval; William mandated an aggressive time line without securing necessary buy-in from key players at the location that drove the most revenue.

I then had several conversations with Jack (whose overriding concern was his location's continued success) to teach him effective mediation techniques in the virtual world. I've learned that friction often occurs when people make their own assumptions that go unchallenged, especially when colleagues work virtually. When colleagues can walk into each other's offices, issues often get resolved through face-to-face discussion—which is not an option in the virtual workplace.

In these circumstances, a structured approach is necessary. It was important for Jack to understand the big picture as well as Leo's and William's individual points of view. He spoke with each of them several times, making note when the two disagreed on specific situations. After Jack and I reviewed the overall situation, he was ready to hold the mediation call by videoconference. I sat in on this call as a consultant/partner, and my role was to watch the mediation process, monitor it, and keep things on track. First, Jack set the ground rules for the call. He explained that as the mediator, his responsibility was to make sure both Leo and William had the opportunity to present their perspectives. They were to keep emotion outside of the conversation and focus on what was in the division's best interest. This is difficult to do, of course, when feelings are running high. This initial virtual meeting lasted over two hours. During this time both men stated their position, and when disagreements arose as to deadlines and available resources, Jack kept probing until they both agreed on what was possible. Finally, both Leo and William restated their positions, and Jack summarized the priorities. Another call was scheduled for the following week to resolve their differences, giving Leo and William time to align possible solutions with the goal of having the new financial system up and running by the new fiscal year.

During the next call, both men presented their plan for action. William agreed to assign several employees from headquarters to Houston for the next few months, and Leo agreed to devote more time to this key project. William also agreed to visit Houston to meet Leo and key managers within the next few weeks, providing an opportunity to establish a better working relationship with Leo. It was also agreed that a weekly videoconference would take place until the end of the fiscal year to monitor deadlines. The result was that the deadline was met and the new system was in place at all locations, simplifying global sales projections and analysis. Leo and William never became close friends, but they did overcome personal differences to meet organizational goals. And that, after all, is the aim of any successful mediation: to ensure that personal differences and underlying conflict do not derail organizational objectives.

Turning Lemons Into Lemonade—Productive Conflict Management

Lemons can taste sour, but added to water and sweetener, they are transformed into a wonderful beverage. Similarly, if you practice productive conflict management, you can turn potentially treacherous and risky situations into successful outcomes.

There are many ways for virtual managers to help mitigate conflict in their teams. The goal is to reduce conflict as soon as a problem is suspected, or before it begins to manifest itself. Anticipating conflict before it surfaces saves time later on, as well as potential expenses caused by work disruptions.

Tips for Handling Conflict Management in Virtual Teams

➤ Prepare employees for conflict; invest in training so that employees will be ready and willing to take ownership of their conflict situations.

➤ Make sure you schedule one-on-one time with each team member on a regular basis, and invite feedback.

➤ Accept conflict as part of organizational life. Observe and acknowledge what has happened. Make it a point to notice what is going on.

➤ Make the first move toward resolving the conflict (i.e., take responsibility) because you do not want the situation to fester or become a stalemate.

➤ Refer back to your Team Setup report (Chapter 2) and the Rules of the Road that you established earlier. You may want to revisit those rules from time to time and refresh the conflict behaviors for which you hold team members accountable.

➤ Communicate about the conflict. Don't hold it in or be afraid to speak up. Express how the conflict makes you feel and how you see it. Reframe the conflict experience in terms of the bigger picture and not just the particular situation.

➤ Encourage employees to speak up and ask for help in resolving conflicts. Coach them to put themselves in the other person's shoes to understand their coworker's point of view.

> ➤ Use a structured approach and common language to address conflicts, and be flexible about possible resolutions.

> ➤ Take care not to confront someone in public (during a conference call, for instance). Address conflicts in private with the appropriate individuals first.

> ➤ Learn from the conflict experience so that you can improve your skills in this area for the future.

> ➤ Above all, choose your battles carefully. Don't let the urgency of a request push you into giving an emotional response. Stay in control of yourself and calmly evaluate requests.

Four Steps for Personally Handling Conflicts

1. Pause before responding.
2. Acknowledge the other person's feelings/reactions.
3. Ask questions. Questioning gives you time to think and gain control. It also may provide you with new data and more clarity on what the other person is saying.
4. Suggest taking a break or continuing the conversation at a later point if you feel you need it.

Note: While your personal response is important, don't take the situation personally. That is, acknowledge your emotions without acting on them, and focus instead on understanding and solving the problem.

How Your Peers Handle Conflicts

"I defuse conflicts quickly. I don't avoid them—I deal with them right away. Once I talk to the team, first, I ask, 'What would it take to get the program on track?' Second, I ask, 'If we could do one thing, what would it be?'"

—GLOBAL LEADER, ELECTRONICS

"I use the three Rs technique: Reflect on the other person's feelings, Restate the underlying issue, and Resolve the conflict."

—VT LEADER, MEDICAL/HOSPITAL ENVIRONMENT

> *"If the conflict is about someone's personality but both team members are doing a good job, I have them work separately but still participate in calls."*
>
> —VT MANAGER, FINANCIAL INVESTOR RELATIONS FIRM
>
> *"To resolve conflict, I shut down e-mail, especially when e-mail is at the center of the storm, and say, 'Let's take it to a public forum and use the phone.' Once you get people talking, 80 percent of the time it can bring down the emotional state and 20 percent of the time, even phone calls don't help because you cannot see people's reactions."*
>
> —SENIOR LEADER, IMAGING COMPANY

Virtual Team Mediation Techniques

Virtual teams have a heightened awareness about the need to pay attention to their processes. In the traditional world, when conflict exists between two team members, you get them in the same room talking about an issue. In the virtual world, you are somewhat limited in your options. Most solutions rely on building virtual bridges to overcome physical distance. Your interactions are limited to phone or video communication, and the connection is surely not as immediate. As one virtual leader in a high-tech company said, "When you have a problem with someone who works in the same building or with a colleague in an intact team vs. a cross-functional team member, you handle it differently because the former is like a family. The solution might be the same [because you still have to bring the team together either face-to-face or virtually to work through the conflict issues], but your approach might change."

One of the themes that I hear repeatedly, both through my consulting work and from the many interviews conducted for this book, is that virtual managers have to learn to become mediators. "I often act as a moderator when there is an argument between team members," says a team leader at a global financial company. "One aspect of being virtual is that people use e-mail instead of the phone and create truth-avoiding conflict. If you were in an office, people would stop by your desk. In the virtual world, people can hide. So I solve problems over the telephone," says a virtual manager at a consumer products company.

When conflict arises between virtual team members, it often has to be mediated over the telephone, a medium that offers advantages as well as disadvantages, as shown in Figure 5-5.

Although conducting a sensitive discussion by telephone is not the first choice, it is the best choice when it is not possible to meet in person. It still allows some level of sincerity and establishes real and direct (verbal) communication with those on the other end of the phone line.

Figure 5-5. Telephone conference call mediation.

Advantages	Disadvantages
• Sometimes it is easier to be honest about an issue when you don't have to look into someone's eyes.	• Without seeing the other person's facial expressions or body language, it is difficult to gauge the person's reaction to your words.
• If someone is shy, the person may feel more comfortable talking over the telephone.	• You can't be sure why someone becomes quiet.
• On the phone, people may feel more comfortable saying something they wouldn't in person.	• Someone can refuse to participate.
• People may be more willing to state an opinion over the phone because it is more impersonal than face-to-face interaction (which is scarier).	• It's possible that conflicting parties may not actually be listening to each other.
	• Conflicts may not be uncovered as quickly over the phone as they would if the team members were meeting on-site.

Mediating Conflict Through a Conference Call

There are several effective virtual mediation tips that I recommend. Before the scheduled conference call, set ground rules for the conversation and be involved as the mediator in the discussion. Your role is to act as a moderator/facilitator/referee, helping people get to their own solutions. You can help prioritize and create alignment between their actions and goals. Many of the managers I interviewed have used the same technique. They hold one-on-one conversations with each team member before holding a joint conference call. These individual conversations are useful for clarifying issues, building trust, and minimizing politics.

Here are some further examples. You do not need to use all of them with your team. Choose the methods that can work for everyone.

Before the Conference Call (Setting Ground Rules)

➤ Recognize that everyone has an opinion about almost everything.

➤ Deal with realistic issues that are solvable.

➤ Acknowledge differences of opinion.

➤ Listen to other team members first; then decide how to respond.

➤ Express feelings and thoughts openly.

➤ Use *I* statements and specific examples.

➤ Be sure that labeling or insulting is off-limits.

➤ Acknowledge that everyone takes responsibility for creating, promoting, or allowing the conflict.

➤ Work together on solutions.

Establishing Your Role

➤ Clarify your role as referee/mediator/moderator.

➤ Clarify your expectations.

➤ Encourage everyone to be honest.

➤ Be fair and impartial—don't take sides.

Guiding the Process

Step 1. Open the discussion effectively without blaming anyone. The goal is to find commonalities and set the stage for open communication and motivated change. Acting as a referee, you are there to call things as you see them. You are not to take sides, but rather be the neutral party and clarify any misunderstandings.

Step 2. Get each person's ideas and input first. Acknowledge all ideas without agreeing or disagreeing with them. Clarify the issues people have and help individuals share information.

Step 3. Present and compare ideas to foster discovery/dialogue and move toward action. Discuss the main virtual conflict issues (e.g., missing information, budget issues, communication style, work product). Clarify what is going on and have people take responsibility, even partial ownership of the issues.

Step 4. Specify actions and gain commitment to plans. Get greater involvement by building cohesiveness; focusing on the issues at hand (not on the people or personalities); and affirming direction, priorities, and plans. Remind teammates that they don't have to be best friends, but they do need to work together. Confirm your support and promote learning from this experience.

Toward the end of the conference call, make sure that you reach some level of problem solving and that all conversations tie back to the goal of the team/project/result. Although their approaches or styles might differ, people actually want similar things. They may argue on the call because they are ambitious or competitive. They may even raise their tone a bit or ignore (back away from) the conflict, but most of the time people want to be part of something, they want to solve the problem, and they want to be successful. As a manager, you are there to facilitate: Engage the conversation; ask the parties to respond; and then, together, find a solution. Here are a few additional tips for handling the call itself:

> Pay extra attention to your tone of voice, to be sure you are conveying the right message.

> Confirm with the other people on the call that your intention is being heard, and do so frequently during the call.

> Eliminate distractions that can take your focus away from the conversation.

> Do not multitask while on the call.

> Listen for cues that may be inconsistent with the words the other person is saying (e.g., Do people hesitate or lower their tone of voice? Do you detect uncertainty in someone's voice? Is anyone saying yes too quickly?).

CASE STUDY

Can Oil and Water Ever Mix?

One client, a virtual manager at a software company, shared this story of virtual mediation:

"Two of my employees had different approaches to getting the work done and a strong lack of tolerance for each other. Mark was a task-oriented project manager: Type A personality, a go-getter, a 'just do it and get it done' guy. Gary was a software developer, a 'wait a minute' personality who was very careful and methodical in his work. They clashed and the relationship deteriorated. Mark kept saying that Gary was not performing, and Gary complained that due diligence was not getting done and mistakes were bound to happen. At first I thought that work was not getting done. I called both of them to find out what each thought the problem was. It turned out that the work was getting done, but there was unnecessary friction along the way. Both individuals stressed that they had trouble getting their message across to the other. Gary, the software developer, didn't express himself in the [way] that Mark, the project manager, wanted him to. I realized that their different communication styles led to this rift. These two people were flamed up with each other.

"Here's the process I took to resolve this situation. First, I conducted several one-on-one sessions with each employee. Second, I then mediated a conference call with both [of them], which began with both employees stating what they wanted to accomplish. Fortunately, they agreed on the end result—a successful project. Third, they discussed the work and agreed that wasn't the issue: The disagreement was about the means to achieving this end; that is, the approach. Fourth, we talked about communicating in ways that [would allow them to] help each other. I said to Mark, 'Okay, when you ask Gary about [a specific issue], it affects him in such and such a way.' Mark then said, 'When Gary says [a specific thing], I think he is not doing the work.' So we had to get beyond the styles and understand how to communicate intentions so that the conversation could improve."

What was the outcome? According to the manager, "They worked on this project until it was completed, and the work continued to get done. They knew they disagreed about style, and it took a continuous effort to keep the communication going. We did that through multiple calls. Once the project ended successfully, Gary and Mark moved on to another virtual project."

What If Your Best Efforts at Mediating Conflict Fail?

If you try to mediate a conflict but cannot resolve it, you may have to separate the parties. Blaming yourself or others wastes energy; sometimes resolution is not possible. If the virtual conflict has festered too long, the parties may not be willing to put the effort into working out the issue, or the project starts moving in a different direction. You may need to find another role for a team member, or even transition an individual out of the team. As one virtual leader at a global consumer products company commented, "If the problem person keeps doing things in the same way after the mediated calls, I separate [the individual] or even manage the person out of the group."

If a toxic conflict still exists, estimate its true cost, including the cost of not meeting deadlines or missing a target date to launch a new product. Compare this cost with the expense of bringing everyone together for an in-person meeting. After you complete the evaluation, if it is appropriate, schedule your meeting.

In a Nutshell—Reducing Virtual Team Conflict

The most productive approach to dealing with conflict in virtual teams is to take steps that actually reduce the potential for conflict *before* it occurs. Teams do this in a number of ways: Team members sensitize each other to their individual preferences; they cross-train to learn and appreciate each other's perspective on tasks; they produce and follow guidelines (Rules of the Road and a Team Code) on how to operate. This last method is simple yet very successful. If team members know, understand, and agree on a set of rules for diffusing conflict, then they will be more effective as a team.

Along with the many other lessons offered throughout the chapter, here are some final tips for reducing virtual team conflict:

> ➤ Continually monitor, manage, and diffuse potential conflict
>   situations.

> ➤ Use the three Ps of conflict resolution to understand the People and the Process involved and the Problem to be solved.

> ➤ Don't pass work on to another team member in a form you wouldn't want to receive it.

> ➤ Don't accept such work from someone else.

> ➤ Assumptions are risky; make them only when you have to.

> ➤ Clarify where your responsibility starts and stops, and how it fits with that of other team members.

> ➤ Update people who need to know what you know.

> ➤ If you have an issue or a point of disagreement with a team member, tell that person, not others.

> ➤ Try to resolve conflicts early (as soon as you sense some tension or misunderstanding).

> ➤ Take time to explain and talk with others about the issues.

> ➤ Seek to understand first before being understood.

> ➤ Strive for open and honest team relations.

> ➤ Turn conflicts into problem-solving opportunities.

Use the following Virtual Roadmap exercise, written as a series of questions, to review the lessons in proactive conflict management offered in this chapter. These questions will help you plan ways to solve problems in the virtual world.

YOUR VIRTUAL ROADMAP TO PRODUCTIVE CONFLICT MANAGEMENT

What types of conflict exist on my team? • Performance • Identity • Data • Social	What steps am I taking to resolve them?

As a team leader, what strategies do I practice regarding conflict management?

What are team members doing to resolve misunderstandings?

What are my team's Rules of the Road regarding conflict management and conflict resolution? (If necessary, once again review Chapter 2 on establishing operational team Rules of the Road and a Team Code.)

What ideas does my team have for team members to post solutions to problems?

Describe a situation where I may need to mediate a tele/videoconference:

What is the situation?	Who are the team members involved?	What are their perspectives?

Date of Call:

• Agenda:
• Ground Rules:
• Discussion:
• Outcomes:

What steps am I taking to create win-win relationships across the organization?

CHAPTER **6**

Getting Deliverables Out the Door

Since delivering results is the most clear-cut of the four elements that define successful virtual teams, you may think it would be the easiest to master, as long as action steps and status checks are in place. However, that is not the case. Although deliverables are measurable, and therefore straightforward, they can become comingled with the other three elements of team success—communication, accountability/trust, and conflict management—and are subject to similar pressures and complexities.

Getting deliverables out the door is specific to the team, and since teams exist to accomplish results, managing the process successfully is an art as well as a science. You haven't reached your destination until you drive your goals. How you approach deliverables (the very reason the team exists) and the specific implementation tools/processes used are going to vary.

This chapter introduces several guidelines to follow in making choices around deliverables. These guidelines are based on my consulting experience and the experiences of the 150-plus virtual team managers I spoke with in preparation for this book. These guidelines seem to work across teams, in spite of each team's unique characteristics. As you read this chapter, consider your own team and the different approaches available to determine which of the suggested practices would work best for your situation, in both the short term and the long term.

What Is Difficult About Managing Deliverables?

Never has the challenge of virtual managers been greater than it is today. Tasks are so far-ranging in structure, technical complexity, and organizational span that the days of the "supermanager" who knew every element of the project inside and out are gone. From day one, the input of team members who bring their special expertise is now integral to solving a business puzzle with many interlocking parts.

All organizations use team projects to translate strategies into actions and to transform objectives into realities. Many teams are project-intensive: They live and breathe project management throughout their life cycle. Organizing around projects is a natural way of life. However, realizing project objectives is not easy when teams are distributed globally and when you factor in intricate technology issues, outsourced work groups, cultural differences, budgetary pressures, and disparate regulatory requirements.

All members of a virtual team, from the manager on, must understand how their efforts impact the deliverables. That, of course, is why they are on the team! Reaching milestones and completing projects require strong support, and as the manager, you are charged with putting a workable structure in place.

The difference between "good" and "great" team management is in the delivery. Strong delivery capability is the result of effective planning, sound processes, and careful monitoring, all of which translate strategy into action. Over the years I've observed many virtual teams, and in every case—no exceptions—they run more smoothly and stay competitive if they plan wisely, maintain ongoing communication among members, and have clearly delineated deliverables.

Conversely, when projects are rife with inefficiencies, the delivery of project results may be hindered. For example:

Inefficiencies That Affect *All* Project Deliverables

➤ Ineffective processes are used for project planning, monitoring, coordination, risk management, and follow-through.

➤ There is inefficient scope management and staff utilization.

➤ Schedules are created in isolation, without integrating key areas of dependency.

➤ Team members do not report steps/actions and accountability breaks down.

➤ Delays in area A are not communicated to area B, which is dependent on area A for its own goals.

➤ Resources are not allocated where they are most needed.

➤ Schedules fail to identify critical paths and do not include nonworking time (and time zones) unique to a particular country/culture.

➤ Key information is not properly documented and/or communicated in a timely manner to stakeholders.

➤ Responsibility for decision making is not clearly defined (e.g., Who decides when a deadline or a priority is changed?).

➤ The fundamentals of proactive communication are not in place.

➤ No risk management plan exists.

➤ Key activities are delayed, forgotten, or changed drastically, without thought given to the impact on other aspects of the project.

In the virtual environment, deliverable management is often about getting work done and moving on. Action-oriented managers are often wary of anyone or anything that may slow them down. They may be more concerned about meeting milestones than developing a strong foundation of structure, process, and tools with which to build future success. That might work well in the short term when the focus is on implementation, but the temporary structure of many virtual teams and the need to move quickly may encourage shortcuts that have long-term costs.

Many virtual managers also fail to realize that team alignment must be addressed not just initially during Team Setup (see Chapter 2), but throughout the entire team life cycle. If meeting deliverables is the objective, whatever your time zone, then successfully completing assigned projects and/or responsibilities depends directly on your ability to foresee pitfalls, design workable processes, and change them when necessary.

In a sense, virtual teams encounter general project management issues similar to those faced by traditional teams, but with the added layers of time and space creating additional demands. These obstacles are challenging, but they can be an advantage, too. Elements special to deliverables on virtual teams are detailed later in this chapter, but to start, let's summarize effective delivery practices.

Checklist: Practices for Effective Deliverables Management

✓ Plan and organize work and schedules by dividing tasks into smaller action steps.

✓ Develop workable communication processes so that progress and problems are easily reported.

✓ When there are multiple projects, break them down so that it is easy for the team to coordinate where necessary and collaborate when the need arises.

✓ Monitor and control costs by building in frequent check-ins.

✓ Report progress and provide early warnings of delays to all stakeholders.

✓ Document and share learnings so that future deliverables benefit from the process.

Checklist: Additional Deliverables Management Practices Relevant to Virtual Teams

✓ Manage projects by communicating clear deadlines that people buy into regardless of their location. Remember that documentation and coordination take on greater importance when physical distance increases.

✓ Strive to make team members more autonomous and self-disciplined so that they recognize when their work is off schedule.

✓ Update communications/documents frequently, and ensure that version control is in place.

✓ Divide tasks into smaller parts/steps/activities, since team members work on various aspects at different times and in different locations.

✓ Direct the team to keep communications flowing continually if team members work across several time zones.

✓ Take immediate action to get back on schedule if things get off track.

✓ Continually check and measure results. Many virtual team managers interviewed for this book offered the same advice: *Follow up, follow up, follow up.* So, do a lot of follow-up.

✓ Document and share new knowledge with teammates. Some virtual managers refer to it as doing an "autopsy" at the end of every project and finding ways to do it better next time.

✓ Strive to understand how deliverables can be affected by different cultural, ethical, and interpersonal values; put the effort into knowing your team.

Deliverables Across Time Zones

"You need to connect your business to everyone!" said Sam, who runs a small electronics company. "When it comes to business, connecting people, linking them from point to point, using knowledge-sharing tools or social networking portals gives you a great way to share your vision and strategy, inspire others, and move deliverables into the customers' hands."

Sam connects to his people daily using wireless technology. He wants to know what they are working on, what they hope to accomplish, and what is actually getting done. Sam looks for measurable milestones in every communication. His direct reports e-mail him at the beginning and at the end of the workday. Because his direct reports manage their own virtual project teams, their time is limited and defined by the miles and time zones that separate them.

Sam's team "follows the sun." People work different hours (in India, the United States, and Europe), and their workday overlaps for a few brief hours. As a result, tasks can take longer to get done due to availability. Often team members work on multiple projects simultaneously and are not fully dedicated to one project, so when something is due, it can get hectic. If an assignment has a tight deadline, then several team members work on it while others sleep, and then they hand their work product off to other members who move the project along. Sam's managers have set up regular checkpoints for when individuals hand a project off to the next person. To accommodate a client who complained about a defective part, several teams worked two days around the clock to resolve the problem. Sam acknowledges that "we spend extra money and time to get the virtual team to work together and produce quality deliverables," but realizes that the geographical distribution allows the workday to span as many hours as necessary, which gives the team an extra advantage. "I can no longer walk down the hall to get the attention of my associate or have a face-to-face meeting," Sam says, "but I found that I can turn this disadvantage into an advantage by being able to produce work continuously, virtually 24/7, even on holidays."

Not every manager shares Sam's enthusiasm. I often hear comments from frustrated virtual managers about working across time zones. One team member may finish work at a given hour and doesn't see the results until late afternoon the next day. This leads to frustration since precious time is lost (a day, an hour) as are opportunities because team members can't "eyeball" each other. Many virtual team managers believe that their costs and benefits should be carefully weighed to determine if the benefits can justify their associated costs.

For Sam, the deliverables challenge is the opposite—remote teams will work until midnight because they can, thanks to technology. And this requires his virtual managers to be involved in important ways: They must clarify expectations and conduct interim reviews (have frequent checkpoints) to quickly catch mistakes. The purpose of frequent check-ins is to shine the light on issues before they cause breakdowns. Your job is to make sure that expectations and instructions are clear up front. "When in doubt," Sam says, "you need to clarify things or you will get something different from what you expected."

Coordinating Deliverables

Coordinating deliverables is like conducting an orchestra. Your job as a virtual manager is to be the conductor who coordinates tasks by planning, by talking, and by tracking. As one virtual team member bluntly stated, "You need to talk about communication, talk about prerequisites, talk about the plans, talk about performance, talk about the breakdowns, talk about solutions—be involved in so much talking that people are sick of talking."

However, successful virtual managers don't just do the talking; they get involved in the listening, questioning, and coordinating. This links back to three behaviors virtual managers need to cultivate for successful deliverable management: (1) aligning, (2) tracking, and (3) establishing frequency of communications.

1. Aligning

The act of aligning is step one in focusing the virtual team to get things done—and to get deliverables out the door. You need to make sure that team members share an understanding about expectations, and that everyone is committed to the same goals. Given the challenges (a culturally diverse team that spans several time zones across dispersed locations), it is even more important to keep team members aligned. Without alignment, teams experience periods of instability, ambiguity, and tension that can lead to a lack of productivity and, eventually, a breakdown of the team itself. Your role, first and foremost, is to guide team members to face the same direction, setting the stage for effective work processes that ensure a strong delivery capability.

Aligning Goals and Expectations Brings Focus

To manage any team, on-site or virtual, establish your goals and expectations, and then create a plan to deliver them. Of course, the virtual world brings a set of circumstances with certain challenges that affect how virtual team members interact during the workday and communicate about projects. As a manager, the more specific your planning is, and the more checkpoints you build into daily activities, the greater your chance of heading a high-functioning team. How else will you know if your intentions were understood as you intended, and how will your team members know if they are on track?

Aligning goals and expectations consists of orchestrating multiple processes and mechanisms, and your role as the team leader is to get the players to play in concert. And while business requirements are often dictated by outside stakeholders, you are like the conductor who makes sure that the orchestra members concentrate on the entire composition as they master their own individual parts.

Tips for Aligning Goals and Expectations

➤ Meet with stakeholders ahead of time to understand important elements: what product/service the team is charged with producing, who will benefit from it, what resources/information the team will need, and what criteria the team will be measured against to evaluate the quality of the deliverables.

➤ Have a project plan with specific specifications. Reconfirm and monitor due dates continually.

➤ Prioritize work at the individual and process level. Identify which tasks are most important and connect them to project goals. Since tasks and priorities change constantly, be ready to refocus and handle changes that vary in priority and scope.

➤ Don't do twenty things in a mediocre way; instead, pick three to five deliverables and do them well.

➤ Create a project summary sheet *before* the project begins.

➤ Clarify when something is due and in what time zone. Give yourself more time for conducting checkpoints and testing in between. Successful virtual managers suggest checking in two or three days ahead of the date when tasks are due.

➤ Use project management software, spreadsheets, and documents. Create scheduled time lines that are broken down into short-term and long-term tasks. Establish and keep schedules for quality reviews and measure the quality of work output.

➤ Reinforce modes of communication for all possible situations.

> Forget control. You don't have any! Virtual members are not like employees—they are like customers. Treat them as such.

Aligning Interests Energizes and Motivates

Do you clearly understand what motivates your team to get deliverables out the door? How can you create a team spirit shared by all? To align team members' energy, find a way to generate shared values and to stimulate interest in jointly working toward a common objective. As head cheerleader (one of your jobs), explain how joint efforts will achieve something of value. When milestones are successfully met, credit the team's synergy as the cause of this success.

The team is motivated to reach milestones when its members are part of the initial conversation, that is, during the Team Setup phase. If that is not possible, because business objectives dictate that deliverables, milestones, and specific procedures are determined beforehand, then you, as the team leader, should look for other ways to involve team members in decisions that affect them. In truth, it is impossible to overstate the importance of communicating and involving team members throughout the life of the project.

Tips for Aligning Team Members' Interests

> Create an open and honest conversational work environment. Start by getting buy-in for the team's direction, as necessitated by business objectives. Plan the work and work the plan. Put in the time, up front, to communicate the importance of alignment and synergy around deliverables. It might require extra time, including conducting phone calls and intense conversations to close the gaps when team members do not work closely with each other.

> During Team Setup, or when new projects are ready to be rolled out, create a *virtual steering committee* as an escalation channel when the team needs realignment or when members feel overworked, frustrated, or burnt out. This body acts as a sounding board, mediating and addressing these issues. It is best to rotate membership to avoid burdening the same people.

➤ When things get out of rhythm and deliverables are steering off track, open communication lines to talk freely about the work/deliverables. Lead this process to self-correct.

➤ Treat team members as unique individuals who develop at their own pace and respond to different work styles and motivators related to their individual experiences and cultures. Learn what motivates the team as individuals and as a group. For example, find out what everyone considers a meaningful way to celebrate completing an important milestone.

➤ Connect with your team often to reinforce goals, vision, and direction, and personalize your communication with each team member.

As one virtual manager in a multinational law firm said, "Basically, I know I have to make everyone establish ownership for our work. I am the project manager, but I don't own it on my own—it is a team project, everyone contributes ideas and has preferences, and we do it together."

2. Tracking

Tracking consists of the back-and-forth reporting, updating, and status checking that are vital to the process of producing deliverables that meet quality standards in a timely fashion. When you focus on tracking you are wearing your logistics hat, coordinating efforts from various places and different work units, and monitoring their status. By doing so, you can identify mistakes or problems early on, increasing the likelihood of prompt resolution. Another benefit of tracking is that it prevents team members from distractions caused by multitasking and inattention. The very act of checking in (i.e., asking for status reports) keeps folks on track and focused.

Tracking allows you to follow the team workflow and capture the process to achieve deliverables. The steps may vary from team to team. Although particular requirements may be broken down differently (by months, weeks, days), the main elements of tracking remain the same:

➤ Establish standards.

➤ Create measurable metrics.

➤ Produce requirements documentation.

➤ Report on the status at regular intervals.

Of course, the unique challenges in the virtual environment are the miles and time zones that separate you and team members from one another. Everyone on the team needs to agree on the process and provide status updates. The more complicated those processes are, the more the owners need to break those deliverables into smaller increments and establish status reporting so that results can be verified. Remember, on a virtual team, when it comes to daily work activities, people can't see what their teammates are doing.

Tracking and Reporting Mechanisms

Throughout my consulting work with various teams and in my research, I repeatedly found that more successful virtual teams tackled the issue of tracking logistics early on. They came up with simple, informal ways to quickly report progress updates.

One manager at an e-commerce firm told me that his team members send a weekly report called the PPP: Progress, Problems, and Plans. Each team member highlights the week's activities by answering three questions:

1. *Progress.* What did you do during the week? What were your accomplishments?

2. *Problems.* What issues came up that concerned you?

3. *Plans.* What do you plan to do about it (to move deliverables along)?

John, a virtual team manager at a software design firm who often managed teams of individuals who were not direct reports, said that managing them was a great challenge because his work was not as high a priority as it would be for a dedicated team. By defining a set of short-term (ninety-day maximum) deliverables, he was able to keep team members on track. He took an aggressive approach and kept the plan short, created a roadmap that was easy to understand, and defined milestones that were focused on results. Individuals gathered quickly, formed their goals, and tackled deliverables immediately. They tracked the following specs:

➤ Business Case (Why am I doing it?)

➤ Responsibilities (What deliverables am I responsible for?)

➤ Basic Schedule

➤ Specific Results

➤ Monthly Review Dates with Senior Management

John found that the three-month approach works very well because (1) projects are highly visible in his organization, (2) deliverables are broken into manageable chunks according to ninety-day plans, and (3) results are easy to track. Besides the motivational elements of a short-term focus, team members received quicker feedback (monthly or biweekly updates with senior management). According to John, the trick is to keep members focused for the short term on clean deliverables, with a quick feedback loop, so it is possible to determine if projects are progressing according to plan. By tracking the work frequently, he can quickly see which projects need help and which ones are more complicated, therefore requiring drastic action (e.g., change in personnel or cancellation of certain subprojects).

In sum, here are the elements of a successful tracking and reporting mechanism:

➤ Charter Statement of Project's Objective Within Stated Time Frame (e.g., three months)

➤ Clear Business Impact

➤ Strong Project Sponsorship

➤ Skilled Team Members

➤ 90-Days' Commitment from Each Person on the Team

➤ Signoff from Each Team Member's Manager for This 90-Day Period

➤ Regular Review Dates Throughout

As John said, "Your time frame and rollout schedule are fixed. You have flexibility to vary resources and to project-manage, but the deadline is fixed. I found that people were okay with that. If the project does not go well, at least the end date is in sight."

Tracking Deliverables on a Spreadsheet and in a Progress Report

Deliverables can be laid out in doable increments in a tracking spreadsheet and a progress report, which should be available for the entire team to access at any time. First, agreement must be reached within the team on how best to break down overall goals into smaller tasks. This can be accomplished by setting quantifiable criteria for each deliverable, spelling out what requirements must be met and how they will be measured. Once you ensure that tasks and detailed substeps are spelled out and all members are on board regarding outcomes and priorities, you are ready to create your tracking spreadsheet.

In the virtual world you need to be *extra detailed* in your expectations. Verify the metrics; redefine time lines; and, if possible, build in extra time to meet deadlines to allow for unforeseen circumstances, resource constraints, and business changes. Tracking should be an iterative process, as more time and energy need to be allotted to confirm and reconfirm processes and activities.

Tracking Spreadsheet. Figure 6-1 is an example of a tracking spreadsheet that keeps track of the team's progress by breaking deliverables down to the task level, monitoring steps by team member and skill. Team members have a clear picture of their goals, status updates, and priorities as time progresses.

To work with this template, first identify the overall goals for the team. Next, break down each goal into the specific deliverables associated with it and determine time lines and deadlines required to achieve

Figure 6-1. Sample tracking spreadsheet.

Team Name:
Project Summary:

Overall Goals:	Deliverables:	Time line:
What is the team trying to accomplish?	What are the specific outcomes related to each individual goal?	What are the deadline(s) for accomplishing each goal?

First Goal: **Duration Needed to Complete:**

Steps/ Smaller Deliverables	Resources Needed	Criteria	Potential Issues	Ways to Resolve	Status/ Priority	Start Date	Due Date	Person in Charge
Break down smaller tasks that fulfill each portion of the goal.	Who (people) or what (information) do you need to get this step done?	What are the requirements that you need to meet? How will you measure?	Anticipate any problems or obstacles you might encounter.	Come up with ways to resolve these problems.	High Medium Low Red Yellow Green	When?	Broken down to 1 week or less	Assign

Second Goal: **Duration Needed to Complete:**

Steps	Resources Needed	Criteria	Potential Issues	Ways to Resolve	Status/ Priority	Start Date	Due Date	Person in Charge

Third Goal: **Duration Needed to Complete:**

Steps	Resources Needed	Criteria	Potential Issues	Ways to Resolve	Status/ Priority	Start Date	Due Date	Person in Charge

the goal. Then, for each goal indicate steps, resources, criteria for evaluating quality, potential issues/resolutions, and dates for status checks. With your team members determine start date, end date, and deadlines for each goal. Consider the resources you need to complete the task and assign the person in charge to promote accountabilities.

Progress Report. The second piece of deliverable tracking involves regular, ongoing progress updates or reports. Regular reporting (e.g., weekly, daily) is an effective way to monitor and measure progress toward team goals—it's how one keeps track of who needs to do what, and when. To help you stay on track, it is helpful to use a common form that all team members update. A good practice is to have the person in charge of a specific task or deliverable update the rest of the team. It also allows you to prioritize important deliverables according to shifting business realities, and update the team when this occurs. Some virtual teams use Microsoft SharePoint Server and project software or other online tracking mechanisms, while others conduct live meetings or chats to reprioritize. Whatever system you choose to track your results and capture decision making, make sure that all team members adhere to it and agree on how it will be implemented.

Figure 6-2 is a simplified progress template you can use to update your team reports. It is a useful tool during weekly team meetings, which can begin with each member reporting the status of current tasks. In this way, everyone has a chance to communicate, and a written record allows everyone to view progress, thus ensuring transparency.

Best Practices for Virtual Team Tracking

> Structure is a must! Create a project specification form that contains tracking and scheduling elements.

> Include reporting in your tracking system. Make sure tasks are linked together so that steps can be well organized and easily managed.

> Create and prioritize your list to include benchmarks and metrics. To measure your outputs and accomplishments, start by evaluating 1) how you move deliverables forward and 2) how well you educate teammates on how to solve problems themselves.

Figure 6-2. Sample progress report form.

Progress Summary:				
Report Date:				
Members:				
Deliverables	Person(s) in Charge	Status	Key Issues: What has been done so far?	Tasks and Next Steps: What still needs to be done?
Key Issues:				
Decisions Required/Made and Key Future Dates/Next Steps:				

> ➤ Rely on shared calendars and e-mail/instant messaging for updates and follow-ups between conference calls.

> ➤ Include specifics in a weekly progress report: report date, project status, project summary, key issues, identified risks, tasks and next steps, decisions required, key future dates, budgeted amount, and accountabilities.

> ➤ Delegate tasks and check that they are completed. If not, pick up the phone and reach people quickly.

> ➤ Create systems, processes, and worksheets to document open issues and follow up.

> ➤ Have the discipline to follow up.

> ➤ Keep things to the point, and in a simple format.

> ➤ Attach additional information regarding quality control, feedback, and reward systems, as appropriate.

3. Establishing Frequencies

Once you align deliverables and set up tracking and reporting mechanisms, you are ready to implement the third and final step: establishing frequencies. Frequency is how often you connect with your team and what processes/procedures are in place to do so. Frequency also relates to the routines and checkpoints you establish to review and reinforce progress. Essentially, frequency is the lifeline that allows you and your team to stay connected and equipped to deliver on expected tasks. One of your key responsibilities as a virtual manager is to implement the team mechanisms necessary to establish frequency in the virtual world.

> "Make sure you have the right communication routines in place and constantly follow up on them. Use technology. My global team uses SharePoint, which has a list with weekly updates—and anyone can see it anytime."
>
> —VIRTUAL TEAM LEADER, HOSPITALITY INDUSTRY

> "Have routines. For example, one of our routines is that at the end of business every Thursday, everyone uploads their deliverables onto a site, so we can all see what's happening. And on Fridays I look at it, and so does my boss. We can see if we have to make changes for the next week."
>
> —VIRTUAL TEAM LEADER, FOOD AND BEVERAGE COMPANY

Frequency: How Often Do You Communicate with Your Team?

Successful virtual teams establish regular routines for updates, discussions, and decisions. They conduct regular calls, create expected checkpoints, and contact team members often to avoid loose ends and ensure they overcome potential problems. These are essential practices. Some virtual teams check in with each other weekly, daily, hourly, and sometimes even more often, using a shared online tool (technology is always the enabler). And although the frequency of virtual team communication varies, the point is that virtual teams must communicate more frequently than on-site teams, and you—the manager—must set the tone.

The rate or frequency of your interaction with team members is a key component of a smooth-running team. One of the top trends I noted from interviewing virtual team managers was about frequency of virtual team communication, which varied significantly compared with on-site teams. Virtual teams report faster feedback loops than on-site teams (17 percent more). When asked about frequency of meetings, 90 percent of virtual team managers interviewed said that team meetings were held weekly, while 8 percent said that some type of team-wide meeting occurred three or more times per week, and 2 percent met less than once per week (see Figure 6-3). Given the speed of communication and deliverables time lines on virtual teams, many virtual members reported that their day consisted of numerous phone calls, an overwhelming number of e-mails (sometimes requiring an e-mail management system), and a generally fast pace. The team should be ready for "hypercommunication," as one respondent called this trend.

A common question, then, is: How often should I communicate with my team? Decisions on what tasks should be communicated to whom, how often, and through what channel depend on various team factors,

Figure 6-3. Team meeting frequency (per week).

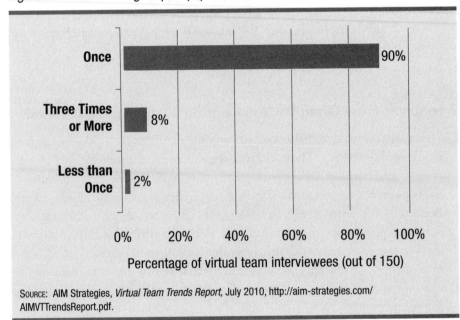

Percentage of virtual team interviewees (out of 150)

Source: AIM Strategies, *Virtual Team Trends Report*, July 2010, http://aim-strategies.com/AIMVTTrendsReport.pdf.

such as team size, degree of task interdependence (or degree of collaboration needed), as well as spatial and geographic boundaries. How you answer this question will likely change depending on life-cycle stage, since deliverables can change over time and directly impact the frequency needed for your team to operate smoothly. Adapt what works for you and tailor the time frames according to your deliverables. Once you clarify the frequency needs around deliverables, you can communicate these requirements to your team.

As one of my clients says, "It is amazing how much can be accomplished in a quick conference call when you set expectations beforehand and tell everyone what you need to accomplish within that time frame."

Figure 6-4 is a sample of a completed table representing choices around frequencies.

Figure 6-4. Frequencies of communication.

Frequency	Task	Stakeholders	Tool
Daily	Individual Status Update, Ongoing Document Review	Everyone	Telephone, E-Mail, or Whiteboards
Daily Subteams	Subtask Update and Discussion	Team Leaders	Online Chat Room or Telephone Call
Weekly	Progress Report Employee Engagement	Team Leaders or Everyone	Conference Calls
Monthly	Progress Reviews Productivity and Results Discussions	Individual and Manager Site Visits with Team Leader and All Members	Videoconferencing
Quarterly	Midpoint Review	Leaders and Design Teams (reconvened and rotating roles)	Telephone or Video
Annually	Comprehensive Review Long-Term Strategy Planning	Everyone	Face-to-Face Meeting (when possible)

Best Practices for Establishing Frequency

➤ Schedule regular communication. Frequency of communication depends on the changing needs of projects and individual work styles. One team member may require daily check-ins, while others can self-manage. Work backward from the master plan and create a project spreadsheet, indicating goals, steps, and priorities. Align the frequency of communication with the needs of each phase.

➤ Outline frequency mechanisms for your team to follow. Be very detailed in your expectations and deadlines. Spell them out! Provide an example of timetables you are looking for (e.g., need to discuss by phone; draft it using e-mail; discuss it again, as needed, during phone/web/videoconference). This alleviates a lot of work later on.

➤ Institute routines so that team members and managers alike are clear on expectations (e.g., How often should they update you? What should team members do when someone is out of the office?).

➤ Balance team members' need for autonomy and the project's need for collaboration.

➤ Create a shared team calendar so that people are aware of target deadlines for executing deliverables. Share task lists and follow-up reports.

➤ Maintain frequent status check-ins. Make sure you communicate constantly and reach out to team members when necessary.

➤ Give your team members the flexibility to self-correct issues while maintaining a strong focus on results.

Frequency and Completion Rates

We have already established that compared to traditional on-site teams, virtual teams need more frequent communication to get deliverables out the door. Increased check-ins are a good idea. However, people often have different definitions of what a "completed" deliverable might look like. I have heard many instances of different perceptions around completion. Here is one particular situation.

Ron M., a telecom client manager in the United States, supervised an English-speaking group based in India, where the business culture was significantly different in terms of hierarchy and structure. Many India-based teams had a top-down management structure.

One high-profile project involved multiple teams developing new telephone software. Status update calls were regularly conducted with team leads, representatives, and developers. From the first calls, Ron noticed that only the team leads regularly talked during the calls, while the developers who wrote code mostly stayed silent. Despite several cultural-learning initiatives, team leaders in India were very resistant to communicating problems with customers, clients, and managers because they did not want to communicate failure. They rarely gave out bad news and always said, "We are working on it" when problems were pointed out.

One team member often said that he was "done" when asked about a specific issue. At first Ron was relieved—until he realized that "done" meant that he "would do it" and the work was not done at all.

Realizing that the Indian developers and U.S. managers did not share the same understanding of the word *completion,* Ron began asking more specific questions and asking them more frequently; for example, "What percentage 'done' are you?" and "When will you complete the next 25 percent?" By asking more explicit questions, Ron avoided a major work delay. He also added a time line and introduced a spreadsheet to identify frequencies and catch mistakes early. As a result, the team improved communications/frequencies and delivered the new generation of telephone software before the launch date.

Virtual managers are faced with a series of complex issues and circumstances that may prevent the team from getting deliverables out the door. Before the situation gets out of hand, you need to administer/implement CPR. In the virtual space CPR (**C** = Communication Plan; **P** = People Plan; **R** = Risk Management Plan) is a planned, systematic approach to keeping things on track so that small issues do not grow, derailing the team's efforts. Consider it your *deliverables survival kit.*

CPR: Communication, People, Risk Management

What does it take for your team to deliver sustainable CPR? It takes designing a relevant and comprehensive tool kit to move deliverables along. Calibrating the elements of this tool kit is no easy task, especially given the paradox that exists in the virtual workplace. Virtual teams call for greater structure than on-site teams, since organizing and sharing information by definition requires structure, yet a flexible approach is needed so that the team easily adapts to complexities/special conditions inherent in the virtual workplace.

Communication Around Deliverables

Effective communication methods allow for the right information to get to the right people at the right time without burdening team members with information overload or excessively complex communication channels. Yet no ideal communication medium exists; each tool and process presents its own strengths and weaknesses. The key to effective collaboration and information sharing is matching the task with an appropriate technology tool. A helpful rule of thumb is to increase the sophistication and richness of the tool/method as the task becomes more complex or the need to collaborate increases. Simpler tools, such as e-mail or phone messages, tend to restrict nuances and prevent contextual clues, especially around elaborate ideas. When information is thus obscured, misunderstandings occur and colleagues may arrive at different assumptions. However, using richer media tools may also present difficulties, since sheer volume of data doesn't necessarily improve communication.

Deliverables Communications Plan

Make your plan broad enough to coordinate information sharing and collaboration around deliverables. Set rules and norms for how communication tools are used, and how frequently, and make sure that team members agree to their use. Consider these factors, among others: team size, number of locations (and time zones), objective(s), and longevity.

Here are some guidelines on how to organize key criteria. When selecting the appropriate communication tools and processes, consider the following questions:

1. *Who Are the Stakeholders?* A stakeholder is someone who influences or is influenced by your team's deliverables. With regard to this plan, the stakeholder is someone who needs to be informed about something as the project takes shape, such as your boss, a colleague, a sponsor, a shareholder, a government official, an executive, a business partner, the press, a customer, a vendor, and of course another virtual team member.

2. *Why Are We Going to Communicate?* What is the purpose of the communication? Generally, working in the virtual space involves receiving, imparting, disseminating, or sharing information, in addition to making decisions and brainstorming. Sometimes the communication has a social element, as we look to deepen a professional relationship through more personal contact.

3. *What Needs to Be Communicated?* What type of information will be shared? It may be short data elements, instructions, questions, complex ideas with granular detail, material that requires further explanation, or some combination of these information types.

4. *When Are We Going to Communicate?* Given a specific set of circumstances, what is the optimum frequency of a specific type of communication (e.g., as needed, daily, weekly, monthly, quarterly, annually)? Always consider time zone differences and cultural preferences, and establish routines according to priorities.

5. *How Are We Going to Communicate?* Complexity, timeliness, and the level of collaboration required all determine the communication medium.

Every organization has its own unique circumstances and challenges; however, the need for solid planning around communication issues is common to all organizations. Let's say you are a virtual manager for a multinational manufacturer and are charged with delivering a new model within a certain time frame. Your virtual team spans several locations throughout the world and may consist of R&D, manufacturing centers, and developers. Based on the needs these questions uncover, creating a deliverables communication plan provides access to key information for everyone.

Figure 6-5 is an example of what your deliverables communication plan might look like. This template breaks down the elements of communication needed to get the deliverables out the door. As you consider your team, use this plan to customize your own in the space provided.

Tips for Developing Your Deliverables Communication Plan

> ➤ Build in a feedback loop at the end of every e-mail, phone call, or videoconference, to ensure common understanding.

> ➤ Propose a time limit for each type of communication beforehand.

> ➤ Take into account the limits of e-mail to convey complex information and the relative skill of stakeholders to communicate in English (the universal business language).

> ➤ As much as possible, consider time zones and what days are off-limits during the span of a key project (bearing in mind cultural, family, or work schedules).

People Plan

Virtual teams are formed for a variety of reasons. Some begin life around a specific project and, as the need evolves, become long-term work units spanning several locations. Others result from deliberate organizational decisions to seek the lowest possible labor and resource costs, regardless of location. Whatever the team's origin, often managers find themselves building and directing members with too little preparation or knowledge. With scant understanding of the unique people dynamics of a globally dispersed workforce, managers are responsible for individuals who are sometimes placed on the team to fill a gap. They do not form a cohesive, productive team, and therefore projects stall and deliverables do not meet quality or budgetary objectives.

Engaging the right people in the right way is a critical component of successfully getting deliverables out the door. Stakeholders include

Figure 6-5. Deliverables communication plan.

WHO	WHY	WHAT	WHEN	HOW
Stakeholder	Purpose	Information Needed	Frequency	Medium/Tool
Sponsor	Share highlights about the project/ progress and gain commitment for decisions and budget	High-level cost, schedule, quality, performance, major problems and planned solutions	Monthly	E-mail, status reports, meeting
Marketing and Sales	Inform key managers about progress in planned sales campaign	Status updates, major roadblocks	Semimonthly	Conference call
Boss	Needs to know	Status reports	Weekly	E-mail, phone contact for problems
Virtual Team Member (IT Project Manager for Project X)	Support for software upgrade	Debugging the program, training	1. As needed— daily at first 2. Weekly (with team)	1. IM or phone calls 2. Conference call
Virtual Team Member (Operations Manager at Manufacturing Facility)	Status report on meeting delivery deadline of product X	Detailed status report on progress toward fulfilling work order	Weekly	Conference call
Virtual Team Member (QC Manager at Manufacturing Facility)	Status report on meeting delivery deadline of product X	Detailed status report on progress toward fulfilling work order	Weekly	Conference call

people both internal and external to the organization with influence on the team. Internal people are your virtual team members who are charged with meeting business objectives; they bring a wide array of skills and experiences. External people may include industry experts, sponsors (such as venture capitalists or others funding the project), as well as the audience or market for the product/service. CPR's focus is on the internal people component—your virtual team members.

Mapping Your Team. Given varying circumstances, what can you, the virtual manager, do to ensure your team's success? Work backward. That is, first consider the nature of the deliverables, their deadlines, and associated budgetary concerns. Then, learn as much as you can about the team members; when face-to-face meetings are impossible, be sure to hold a phone conversation with each team member. Take a quick inventory of relevant information, including their expertise, prior experience, and potential risks, if any, associated with their presence (i.e., the person brings poor communication skills). Are there gaps in needed skills? If so, what training or additional resources are needed? A critical responsibility is to elicit top performance from the team, and it's hard to do that without knowing what motivates each team member. Many studies show that compensation is not the top driver of performance—recognition is. Also, ask people (don't assume) what mode of communication they prefer. Figure 6-6 is a template to map key information about the individuals on the team so that you can make informed decisions about maximizing their efforts.

Playing Your Role. When you are responsible for a dispersed team, the people-management aspect of your job becomes critical. An awareness of what drives people and what presses their buttons keeps work progressing. Flexibility is important. By observing how the team functions, you can restructure or improve processes to create the best circumstances for collaborative teamwork. Successful virtual managers develop their internal radar to know who needs special coaching and when they need it.

Additionally, those who are sensitive to individuals from other cultures can sometimes prevent small issues from escalating. Chances are your team (or teams) may be tasked with simultaneous activities that re-

Figure 6-6. Mapping team information.

Member	Relevant Experience, Skills, and Attributes	Training and/or Developmental Needs	Motivators	Preferred Communication Style	Key Responsibilities

quire many hands to complete. As one virtual manager in an IT organization said, "People know when you're just going through the motions. I take responsibility for meeting our department's goals, but I give everyone else as much leeway as possible in working out how to get there. And I make sure that each individual feels respected."

Lastly, it is important to note that although team members are charged with moving deliverables along, you, as the leader, bear the major responsibility for making that happen. What can you do to keep a healthy perspective and to manage stress and the relentless pressures that come with the job?

You start by determining each team member's most important responsibilities, and organizing them in terms of each deliverable and deadline. For each deliverable, that means addressing the following questions:

> ➤ Who has authority to make decisions?

> ➤ In the case of shared responsibility, do colleagues agree about each other's role, and have they worked out appropriate communication plans?

> ➤ What are acceptable performance standards?

> ➤ What is your reward system? Does the team celebrate successes and acknowledge contributions?

> ➤ Which deadlines and milestones are negotiable and which ones are firm?

Although it is impossible to totally eliminate these concerns and pressures, by following the guidelines for CPR, you will be in a stronger position to tackle common issues in the virtual world.

Risk Management Plan

"Expect the unexpected." Virtual managers live the truth of this statement, given the uncontrollable variables in the virtual space that add to the challenges of an increasingly complex business environment. Even when threats cannot be foreseen, a risk management process should anticipate those that might possibly arise. Unfortunately, a systematic risk management process is too often overlooked because of time constraints and lack of resources; however, ignoring the need to develop one may lead to wasted time, effort, and resources. Risks arise from many internal sources in addition to external ones. Were original budgets arrived at in haste (and therefore overly optimistic)? Was the team put together without sufficient thought to roles and responsibilities? Are resources inadequate to complete tasks? Have poor communication mechanisms led to conflict, quality issues, and missed deadlines? Has scope creep set in, such that the original project has expanded beyond the team's comfort zone and ability to execute?

To begin managing project risk, ask these basic questions:

> ➤ What could negatively or positively affect the project?
> ➤ What is the likelihood that this situation may occur?
> ➤ How will it impact the project?
> ➤ What can be done to mitigate its adverse effects?

The answers to these questions will prepare you for developing a risk management plan.

Identify, Analyze, and Prioritize Potential Risks. Formally or informally ask stakeholders to identify potential threats, both internal and external. As the manager, you need to analyze items by severity and probability to prioritize them. How will they ultimately impact the schedule, cost, quality, people involved, and mix of skills needed? For example, if your deliverable depends on timely software upgrades, is the outsourced vendor reliable? Should you consider a backup? With whom should you be brainstorming to determine the probability of this event occurring, and what measures will you put in place to mitigate it? Review and add to this list regularly.

Assign Ownership for Risk Strategies. Consider who is responsible for which risk and discuss which strategy is appropriate. There are four possible risk strategies, depending on the severity of the threat:

1. *Accept.* Accept the possibility of X occurring. Do not put corrective action in place; plan to monitor its impact. This works well for small risks.

2. *Transfer or Share.* Once the issue has been identified, contract with another party to share the risk. This goes to the very heart of how business is conducted in high-risk, costly operations, such as large-scale construction.

3. *Reduce or Mitigate.* Reduce the likelihood or severity of the risk. Either adjust a process, extend a deadline beyond what was initially considered, or build in extra checkpoints.

4. *Avoid.* Eliminate or withdraw from the risk. While the project is in its early phases, choose an alternative approach that does not involve that risk. Some projects, by definition, preclude this option as they deliberately invoke high risks in the expectation of high gains. However, this is the most effective technique, if applicable.

Create the Plan. Now you are ready to develop an actual risk management plan. It must consist of these five elements:

1. *Prioritize the Risks.* List all potential risks in order of descending potential impact (consequence) or likelihood (probability of occurrence). The likelihood of the risk occurring ranges from virtually impossible to absolutely certain, while the consequence varies from negligible to catastrophic.

2. *Describe the Threats/Risks.* Be as concise as possible, but not so concise that team members cannot identify the issue.

3. *Describe the Impact.* If the threat were to occur, its potential consequences might affect, for instance, cost, time line, or product quality.

4. *Identify the Owner.* Name and provide contact information for the team member who is responsible for monitoring and communicating the risk to the team or, if authorized, for responding to the situation.

5. *Describe the Response Strategy.* Briefly describe actions to be taken in response to the threat. (They involve accepting, transferring, reducing, or avoiding.)

Figure 6-7 is an example of a risk management plan for a high-tech manufacturing firm.

Figure 6-7. Risk analysis matrix.

Priority	Description	Impact	Owner	Response Strategy
1.	Change in currency rates would impact net income for the division	Negatively or positively affect manufacturing costs and competitiveness of products	Manufacturing Project Leader	Avoid—Change supplier, decrease overall costs of product (could affect quality)
2.	Change in ownership of key software vendor	Potential delays in software updates	IT Director	Consider bringing development in-house

Tips for Managing Risk

> ➤ Identify risks/threats that affect objectives (whether positive or negative).

> ➤ Plan a coordinated application of resources to minimize, monitor, and control the impact of unfortunate events.

> ➤ Make decisions based on the best available information, and take into account the human factors, such as personal characteristics, cultural influences, and skills.

> ➤ Tailor decisions to your team dynamics and be transparent and inclusive.

> ➤ Be systematic and structured in your approach.

> ➤ Respond to change promptly and swiftly.

While responses to handling risk differ, the only ineffective approach is to deny its possibility, and therefore to do nothing.

Realignment: Refreshing Your Team's Deliverable Management Strategy

Successful teams conduct periodic check-ins to review overall goals/strategy, refine the mission, improve processes, and handle shifting priorities. In virtual teams in particular, reviewing incremental steps is vital. As we know all too well, conditions change and surprises occur, and agile virtual managers must know how to quickly realign the team.

Realignment is similar to "refreshing" your team and performing the maintenance that enables teammates to refuel, tune up, and redirect their energies. Part of the realignment process is motivating members to keep them involved in everyday activities. In an ideal situation, periodic in-person meetings are used to cultivate connections. But if that is not possible, conference calls or webcasts can substitute. For optimal results, set a structured agenda to support the realignment process and focus your team on current priorities.

As a global manager at a pharmaceutical company said, "Realignment involves cycling and recycling through overlapping phases. I must create time for my team to reflect and recycle. This requires periodic get-togethers to see where we stand, discuss current issues and concerns, agree on where we are going [next steps], and decide how to adapt accordingly. Taking corrective action underlies staying on track and allows for the flexibility that permits easier, continuous realignment."

When realigning your team during an in-person or virtual meeting, first take the time to reinforce what is going right with the team. That is, acknowledge your team's results and past accomplishments. Then, discuss the changes in the business environment that make adjustments necessary. The structured agenda should be to rescope short-term targets; review, revise, and realign measurable goals; engage in brainstorming activities around opportunities and threats; and agree on follow-up actions and time frames. During the process, also consider new ways to involve your sponsors, stakeholders, and customers.

Checklist: Key Considerations When Realigning the Team

✓ Has the business environment changed? If so, how are you adapting to it?

✓ Have your stakeholders changed their expectations or priorities about the deliverables?

✓ Have you integrated feedback and lessons learned from the progress report? What can the team improve?

✓ What elements need to be realigned?

✓ Are team members in the most appropriate roles—should roles and responsibilities shift?

✓ What distractions exist that may impede collaboration?

✓ Are productive relationships being built? If not, consider what should be done to implement them.

✓ Is learning being transferred across multiple levels and functions?

✓ Are the proper tools in place to manage, plan, and track the work?

✓ What are you doing to reinforce the processes that are working well and adjust the ones that are not?

Postmortems: Lessons Learned on the Front Lines

Postmortems are an integral part of the process of getting deliverables out the door, particularly when approached from the perspective of improving some aspect of the project or a similar one. It's important for managers and team members to take stock when a project ends and assess what went well and what didn't, so the next assignment benefits from this knowledge.

How best to do this? First, communicate the reason for conducting this review and what you hope will result from it. Stress the need for honesty, and reassure people that punishments and rewards are not forthcoming.

Following is a list of recommended questions that you should distribute to your team in advance of the postmortem meeting. These questions can generate discussion about what went well (or not), and what the team would do differently moving toward the next milestone. I suggest using what I call a +3/–3 process when evaluating projects and conducting postmortems. Discuss three things that went well and three things that could have been improved. After the meeting, summarize key points in a "lessons learned" list that everyone shares.

Postmortem Questions

> What went well and should be repeated/improved in the future?

> What was the single most frustrating aspect of working to get our deliverables out the door?

> What could we do in the future to avoid this frustration?

> Which of our internal methods (i.e., the team Rules of the Road) *helped* this project along?

> Which of our internal methods *hindered* this project?

> What else went wrong and should be avoided in future projects?

> ➤ If you could change anything/one thing about this project, what would it be?

> ➤ Do you feel that stakeholders, senior managers, clients, and sponsor(s) participated effectively? If not, how can we improve their participation?

> ➤ How could we have improved our work processes for creating deliverables?

When evaluating deliverables, keep in mind that mistakes are inevitable, especially in a constantly multitasking world. So it is best to anticipate mistakes and foster an environment that tolerates them. To increase collaborative work, establish an evaluation system that is based on group, not individual, performance. As a leader, make sure you conduct regular check-ins with your sponsors to update progress and to ensure that the team is not drifting. If progress is lagging, add elements to correct the situation. At every opportunity, manage communications, people, and risk (CPR).

One virtual leader at an insurance company sums up the value of the postmortem process: "When we conduct postmortems, I take no chances and make no assumptions when reconfirming my team's understanding and commitment, as well as tracking progress toward ensuring that deliverables are rolled out successfully. It requires a lot of coordination work since people have different standards, but it is worth it in the end."

YOUR DELIVERABLES VIRTUAL ROADMAP

PART 1: What Rules of the Road (internal methods) does your team practice regarding deliverables?

Overall Goals:	Deliverables:	Time Line:
What the team is charged with accomplishing	Specific outcomes related to each individual goal	Deadline(s) for each goal

ALIGNMENT CONSIDERATIONS:

- Do team members know the purpose of our work and its impact on the organization?
- As the manager, do I clearly understand what constitutes the team's responsibilities and what is within our scope/boundary?
- Do members of my team take a collaborative approach to deliverables?

TRACKING:

Deliverables	Person in Charge	Status	Key Issues: What has been done so far?	Tasks and Next Steps: What still needs to be done?

Decisions Required/Made and Key Future Dates/Next Steps:

_____

_____

_____

_____

_____

_____

_____

_____

_____

_____

FREQUENCY:

- Based on my current deliverables schedule, how often must I meet (virtually) with my team?
- How long or how short do these check-ins have to be?
- Do certain topics call for different types of meetings (e.g., longer in duration, more frequent)?
- What technologies/tools do we have available to meet regularly?
- According to the delivery cycle of key deliverables, are there periods that we need to be in closer contact with each other?
- How do we handle time zones and planning/framing frequencies?

Frequency	Task	Stakeholders	Tool
How often we need to communicate about the task	The activity that needs to take place, broken down into individual tasks	Participants in the activity	Medium/method for sharing information

PART 2: Your Deliverables CPR Survival Kit

COMMUNICATION PLAN

WHO	WHY	WHAT	WHEN	HOW
Stakeholder	Purpose	Information Needed	Frequency	Medium/Tool

PEOPLE PLAN

Mapping Your Team					
Member	Relevant Experience, Skills, and Attributes	Training and/or Developmental Needs	Motivators	Preferred Communication Style	Key Responsibilities

RISK PLAN				
Risk Analysis Matrix				
Priority	Description	Impact	Owner	Response Strategy

PART 3: Realignment

- Are deliverables in line with your team's overall goals and vision?

- Has the business environment changed? If so, how are we adapting?

- Have your stakeholders changed their expectations or priorities regarding deliverables? How so?

- Have we integrated feedback and lessons learned from our progress report? What can we improve?

Postmortem, Lessons Learned

- What went well and should be repeated/improved in future projects?

- What went wrong and should be avoided in future projects?

- What was the single most frustrating part of our project?

- What could we do in the future to avoid this frustration?

- Which of our internal methods (i.e., team Rules of the Road) helped this project along?

- Which of our internal methods hindered this project?

- If you could change anything/one thing about this project, what would it be?

- Do you feel that stakeholders, senior managers, clients, and sponsor(s) participated effectively? If not, how can we improve their participation?

CHAPTER 7

Cross-Cultural Communications and Virtual Teams

Today's organizations require people at all levels who can comfortably interact with cultures other than their own. In our shrinking world, as people from various backgrounds and cultures increasingly work together, the need to communicate through a global lens becomes vital. Winning or losing competitive battles depends on operations that function productively abroad as well as at home, and that entails molding successful practices that work well across many cultures. In no area is this need for cross-cultural communication (CCC) more critical than with virtual teams. Team members bring invisible cultural roots that influence behavior around beliefs, values, perceptions, expectations, attitudes, and assumptions. Managers may find that these cultural differences pose special problems that they did not anticipate. The good news is that many virtual managers like you have developed capabilities to overcome these difficulties.

Whether team members work across the street, across the country, or across the world, issues related to CCC exist, even if they lurk in the background. Your virtual team may not be a global team, but chances are that it is a cross-cultural one, and so you have to figure out how to communicate in this world of diminished cues.

Pepper Pot Soup

When teams assemble people of diverse cultures, their differences can create misunderstandings, but commonalities can also be uncovered, as I learned. For many years I taught at New York University and ran an activity called Pepper Pot Soup. Grouped by ethnic backgrounds, students had to describe cultural traits that differentiated them from other cultures. Then I divided the class into random groups of mixed cultures; each group made a hypothetical "soup," noting how their own cultural differences affected their soup recipe. Within the context of the workplace, for example, these differences might be around decision making, teamwork, or independence.

Every class concluded that despite our differences, we all share the most important human characteristic—the need for communication. These differences make the soup more flavorful and open up conversations. Just as ingredients add their special zest to a soup, complementary ingredients can create strong organizations.

Pepper Pot Soup got its name from a Caribbean student whose grandmother made a wonderful stew that filled the house with a peppery smell. She said this soup was not just a meal; it was also like a medicine. And then she made a perceptive remark that I have shared with every class since: Sometimes combining ingredients yields much more than the sum of their individual characteristics. The message was clear that a multicultural organization has a great deal to offer, and its members do not have to shed their differences.

Culture and Communication

At its most basic, culture refers to a group, or community, whose members share similar experiences, worldviews, and values. Up until a few generations ago, most managers worked solely with local counterparts who shared similar backgrounds. Now, in a typical workday, you probably communicate with colleagues, clients, and vendors from different parts of the globe. Language barriers and different worldviews and experiences can cause communication challenges, which can be costly if not overcome. As the pace of business transactions quickens, the ability to communicate with and manage people from other cultures becomes a requirement for success.

Culture is the way we do things. It's how we behave as individuals and in teams. Culture is shaped by our experiences and influences the way we view and understand the world around us. It influences (1) our values and what we consider desirable/undesirable, (2) the behaviors we consider acceptable/unacceptable, (3) our morals around right/wrong, and (4) how we view and interpret the world.

Consider a group of people who share a similar background that consists of patterns of communication, viewpoints, expressions, and behaviors. Taken together, they form blueprints collectively known as cultural patterns; when people refer to other cultures, they generally refer to these cultural patterns. The danger with cultural patterns is that they can lead to stereotyping people, professions, and ethnic groups. Generalizations and stereotyping differ. Stereotypes tend to be negative statements emerging from perceptions about a few individuals that are then applied to an entire group. Generalizations are claims based on thoughtful analysis.

While stereotyping is undesirable, making generalizations about a cultural attribute can help you understand another culture, creating a foundation for a relationship. The materials and action steps presented in this chapter use these cultural generalizations as starting points to help you better understand other cultures and their stories. Please note that these generalizations are not intended to imply that everyone from a specific culture shares certain characteristics or acts the same way. No doubt, as opportunities to interact increase, we will gain greater knowledge about our cohabitants on this planet.

This chapter defines culture as including the shared mental programs that condition individuals' responses to their environment: the collection of values, beliefs, symbols, and norms that members follow. It is based on common experiences that we share with a particular group. Furthermore, it is both learned and enduring—some aspects of culture are built into institutions, while others are passed down through generations. Last, culture is a filter that influences behavior, often in ways that elude our consciousness.

Since culture envelopes us, we adapt to it without realizing that we are doing so. When engaging cross-culturally, we know something is different, but we are often reluctant to discuss cultural characteristics, especially in business situations. And yet virtual managers need to recognize cultural characteristics and understand how they can be used productively to drive business success.

You don't have to walk a mile (or kilometer) in someone else's shoes—but you need to learn to communicate through a cultural lens. This chapter offers tools, tips, and techniques for effective CCC. I will also share another perspective around cultural interactions that I found particularly relevant to virtual teams.

The Intercultural Disconnect

Miscommunications can occur even when core values are shared. Imagine, then, how many more obstacles we face when communicating with parties from different cultural backgrounds. Before we dive into strategies to offset these potential issues, here's an example of how misunderstanding cultural cues can lead to unwarranted conclusions.

Scenario: Will You Hire Him?

Bocci's Tool and Die Company, located in San Diego, California, is hiring three production workers. The recruiter is ready to screen his next applicant. Suddenly the door opens and a dark-skinned young man walks in. Without a glance at the recruiter he finds the nearest chair and, without waiting to be invited, sits down. Making no eye contact with the recruiter, he stares at the floor. The recruiter (born and raised in the United States) is appalled at what he deems inappropriate behavior. Even though the job requires manual dexterity, and strong social skills are not needed, this young man has no chance to meet the production manager. He is cut from the applicant pool before he can step inside the factory door.

You can see how an individual's cultural background affects behavior and perceptions. Most Americans would find this young man's behavior strange or rude. However, he is Samoan, and in his culture it is not appropriate to speak to, or even make eye contact with, authority figures until they invite you to do so. You do not stand while they are sitting, because to do so would put you on a physically higher level than they are, implying serious disrespect. Viewed through his cultural lens, the young man behaved appropriately.

This example illustrates how a person's cultural background (or "cultural lens," as I refer to it) affects behavior and perceptions. Intercultural situations present many opportunities for us to misconstrue others' intentions and in turn embarrass ourselves or our coworkers. This happens because we are often unaware of our own cultural biases. We can also feel threatened or uneasy when interacting with people from different cultures, especially if we are unfamiliar with behaviors that seem inappropriate in a given situation.

The Four Communication Challenges in the Virtual Environment

Let's look more closely at some challenges presented by CCC and the potential for miscommunication.

1. *Lack of Informal Communication.* On-site coworkers have the advantage of communicating informally through the grapevine. Although grapevines may have a dark side, such as allowing rumors to circulate, they do serve a valuable social function. Grapevines give managers and staff a source to tap into information that may not be circulated upward and a channel to leak information downward. Virtual teams that communicate primarily by e-mail have fewer options for informal communication, which means fewer opportunities to correct wrong impressions.

2. *Differences in Perception.* Psychological noise occurs when the message receiver perceives a different meaning from what the sender

intended. How different individuals perceive the same sensory information can vary tremendously, which may result in faulty communication. A further challenge in a virtual environment is the need to constantly double-check how well our message was understood.

3. *Differences in Status.* People occupying different levels on the organizational hierarchy may have difficulty communicating with each other for various reasons. Managers may not adequately value the knowledge of lower-status employees, and these employees may resist sharing negative information with managers, especially if the manager is from another culture.

4. *Differences in Interpreting Context.* In some cultures the words alone convey an individual's intention, while in other cultures the context of the message provides cues that are just as important as the expressed words. In *high-context cultures,* context plays a large part in how to interpret a message, while in *low-context cultures* the words themselves are most important in interpreting a message.

Individuals from low-context cultures typically lack skill in noticing and interpreting background cues. They tend to talk more and depend on verbal rather than nonverbal codes, and they are decidedly uncomfortable with silence. Emphasis is placed on being direct, and the person on the receiving end of the message is meant to respond accordingly. The task is more important than the relationship, so low-context speakers will use clear language, and lots of it, to get their point across.

Individuals from high-context cultures place emphasis on trust and rely on nonverbal communication, so they tend to be less verbal and more comfortable with silence and reading between the lines. Often the words are identical to those from low-context cultures, but another meaning is attached to them. For example, a Japanese businessman might say "yes" when asked if he agrees with a proposal, but in reality he is merely conveying his own understanding—he does not mean that a deal is imminent.

Figure 7-1 shows the world's major cultures on a scale from high to low context.

Figure 7-1. Context scale of different cultures.

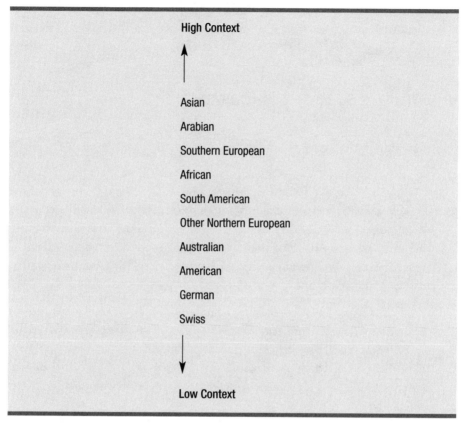

Language Is My Starting Point

All cross-cultural interactions occur through written or oral language. Therefore, when coaching managers of cross-cultural teams, language is my starting point, since it is the basis of communication. After team members identify their country of origin, we look at their cultural characteristics, paying close attention to commonalities and differences in language. We discuss how language can lead to misunderstandings and possibly to conflict. Together we create a plan that considers the types of misunderstandings that arise from these differences and some concrete ways to lessen their negative impact on the team's performance.

Consider the following scenario of a client engagement with a major international telecom firm, where I was brought in to help with interpersonal issues that caused slippage in key target dates during the quality control (QC) stage of a new billing system.

CASE STUDY

"They're So Nice, It's Too Much"

Ted, the virtual team manager, coordinated weekly team meetings from his office in New York without having met any of his overseas team members in person except for a brief meeting in Bangalore with a team led by Kumar. "They're so nice," Ted told me, "that it's too much. I told Kumar to let me know ASAP if he had a problem, since we have some pretty tough characters on our team. I had a sense early on that I wouldn't know what was really going on there because some unpleasant e-mails were directed at [Kumar's] team and he didn't explain what happened or defend the developers or even ask for a more civil tone in future e-mails."

Ted asked me to silently participate on a teleconference call held to brainstorm ways to connect this diverse team. Team members checked in from India, Israel, and other cities in the United States, across many time zones: There were developers from San Francisco, contractors from Bangalore and Haifa, and QC specialists from Atlanta. Here is a summary of what transpired during this call:

- Ted kicked off the meeting by welcoming everyone, and then he detailed the issues related to the software.
- One of the developers from California asserted: *The bottom line is that we are the customer.*
- Someone on the India team followed that comment with this one: *Of course you are the customer.* As the conversation continued, it was clear that India-based team members were very polite and subservient, almost too polite, constantly apologizing for any mistakes.
- Israeli team members found every opportunity to repeat: *That was not our responsibility.* California team members methodically asked for documentation for activities and specific time lines.

When the call ended, I debriefed the meeting with Ted. He summed up his team's characteristics in this way:

American Team's Cultural Characteristics
- They don't think in terms of only black or only white; everything is a shade of gray.
- When a question is asked about an issue they don't know about, team members will say, "Sorry, I don't know, but give me some time to check."
- Generally they don't make a commitment until things are in place.

Indian Team's Cultural Characteristics
- Everyone is extremely polite and subservient in how they talk to us.
- When I get off our weekly conference call, I never know what they really think.
- During our teleconferences, they come across as extremely status conscious.
- They apologize for any mistake, even if it's a minor grammatical error.

Israeli Team's Cultural Characteristics
- Everything is a negotiation with them, whereas with India it's "Yes sir."
- They come across to their peers in California as very rude, almost to the point that if the client wasn't getting a good deal they'd consider dropping them as a vendor.
- They think in terms of black or white, not gray.
- They don't know how *not* to answer. They will commit first and check later whether it's possible.

Knowing that these cultural characteristics created problems around communication and accomplishing goals, I worked with the team (approximately a dozen members) to come up with a series of initiatives, some of which were easy to roll out immediately and some that would require extensive planning.

1. Each team member picked a partner from another region and committed to one phone call each week to discuss one difficult aspect of the project. The call was to last ten to fifteen minutes, and certain ground rules were to be observed: The conversations would take place within a zone of trust, meaning that no one could show impatience at any time. They would be mutually respectful of each other. Questions had to be specific, with concrete answers in response. And, finally, each call would end with an invitational phrase, such as: "What else would you like me to know about XYZ?"

2. Team members agreed to raise the level and frequency of communication about deliverables and due dates. They also committed to pointing out what wasn't clear at the time the interaction occurred.

3. To help deal with cultural differences, the team would exchange members for temporary assignments of three to six months, whenever possible, with Haifa and Bangalore exchanging representatives with Atlanta and San Francisco, respectively.

4. Although travel throughout the division was kept to a minimum, each location would send one representative team member to New York for a two-day meeting every six months. Agenda and criteria for selection would be determined later.

Within the next few months things improved. The team created general guidelines for communicating across the diverse cultures represented on the team. Each week one team member was assigned, on a rotating basis, to summarize the call, noting in a group e-mail the issue, deadline, and responsible party. I was happily surprised when they came up with the idea of devoting the first five minutes of their calls to have one team member, again on a rotating basis, teach the others about one aspect of that person's culture—a holiday, a tradition, or an important event.

CASE STUDY

Pay Close Attention . . .

Language differences entwined with cultural nuances create some interesting situations. Alex, an interviewee who manages a virtual team of data analysts, told me this story about a frustrating situation that he resolved with a workaround:

"I manage a team of five people, so there are usually six of us on any given call. Three of my guys are in Romania, another Romanian is in Florida, and I work in Sydney with the fifth member of my team. When I first managed the team I decided to start each week with a conference call, and that the time would vary to accommodate the different time zones.

"I'll never forget my first call, when I wanted to welcome everyone. I asked George, one analyst in Romania, how he was doing and he said he was fine, so I next asked Aurel, who worked with [George], how he was. But Aurel didn't answer, so I said something like, 'Can you hear me? Are you there?' Silence. 'Are you there?' I repeated. Still no answer. So I asked George [who was in the conference room with Aurel] why Aurel didn't respond. He said, 'Because he does not have a microphone.' But I knew they were both at the same conference table, and I assumed they were sitting right next to each other, so I couldn't understand why George just didn't pass the microphone to him—it's no big deal, but they were so *literal* in their thinking. I was talking to Aurel, so George didn't think it was his place to help out. They lost the commonsense aspect to communicating because they were busy interpreting my exact words. I realized that it was better to use chat and any type of written communication with the Romanian team instead of the phone. If I write something that is unclear, they can look up the meaning in the dictionary and have a written record of it.

"I see this same issue in India and Russia, where they take things literally to a degree that someone more fluent in English doesn't, but they do the specifics of their own jobs really well and with a great attention to detail. For example, if I were to say 'Cut this tree down,' they will do it well and precisely, but if I say, 'Cut a circular driveway,' they don't get it. They're great at zeroing in on the details but flounder when it comes to the big picture.

"It's all about how information is interpreted. Part of it is cultural, part of it is not being in the same room, and part of it is language. My answer for this is to pay close attention to make sure they understand my intention, and to know where they are at any given point on an analysis, especially when a big deadline looms."

Alex's commonsense lessons are worth repeating for virtual managers:

- Pay close attention both to what is being said and to the cultural nuances that team members bring with them. Just as Alex came to understand that he had to hear his own words through the cultural lens of the colleagues with whom he spoke, you have to consider how your words are interpreted by each member of your team. Avoid colloquialisms and keep your instructions specific.
- Know which communication mode to use with each team member. As Alex discovered, written communication worked best with some team members.
- To this advice I would also add that when deadlines are close or situations are critical, you need to check in more frequently and ask appropriate questions to keep the workflow on track. You may be asking for A and getting B, and things can get lost in translation.

When Things Get Lost in Translation

In the virtual world, even when you and your cross-cultural partner speak the same language, it's possible to get lost in translation. This occurs when (1) different meanings are attached to the same words, causing interpretations to vary, and (2) a common expression in one culture is a non sequitur in another. Without clarifying your intention, these misunderstandings can snowball.

I know firsthand how English words may have dual meanings, as an incident with a client that occurred during the planning stage of this book shows. My client was a retail company with several overseas locations. As part of a group e-mail, my office manager and I often requested information about customized materials. In response to a request she made about printing training guides locally, she received this e-mail: "As you demanded, I am sending information about the printing schedule."

She quickly dashed off her own e-mail: "Just for the record, and for your own communication in English, saying 'as you demanded' is not PC! LOL. 'As per your request' would sound much better."

She received this response: "What is PC? Are you referring to our computers?"

At that point she phoned our contact and clarified the difference between the words *demand* and *request*; in addition, she explained that PC in this instance meant politically correct, not a computer. Fortunately, we all had a good laugh and agreed to take extra care with future e-mails.

Virtual Teams Translate English to English

As we have seen, the mix of cultures can cause various obstacles to communication. According to my virtual teams study (see Figure 7-2), the most common difficulty pertains to differences in understanding the English language (as indicated by 47 percent of survey respondents). There are difficulties related to levels of competency, differences in interpretations, literal translation issues, lack of language skills (as happens when team members are hired for technical expertise), and accents. As you can see from the stories shared by my interviewees, even words such as *yes* or *done* can mean different things in certain cultures.

Figure 7-2. Global obstacles to communication.

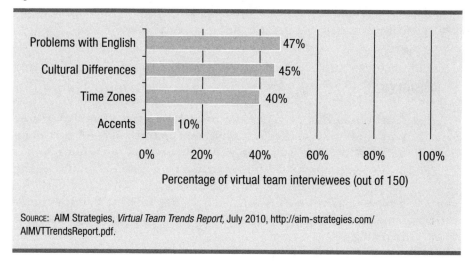

SOURCE: AIM Strategies, *Virtual Team Trends Report,* July 2010, http://aim-strategies.com/
AIMVTTrendsReport.pdf.

You may have seen firsthand that differences in cultures lead to alternate interpretations of events as well as words. Expressions and idioms that are ingrained in one culture lose their meaning when translated and may cause misunderstandings, even if/when we speak the same language. The same holds true for jargon and humor, additional layers that add complexity in cross-cultural communication. Sometimes people from different cultures may not even realize that a difficulty exists, and that's when things really get complicated. Here are some stories from my personal experience and from numerous interviews about situations when things got lost in translation. Perhaps you have experienced something similar on your virtual team.

Saying Yes. One of my clients who worked for a bookseller told of a particularly frustrating situation with a web design vendor. Diane was located in New Jersey while the vendor was in India. Prior to a big launch, Diane held weekly calls with the designers to review agenda items, projected due dates, and potential issues. Her questions were always met with a pleasant, earnest "Yes," but deadlines continually slipped and calls and e-mails were not answered. She was forced to place multiple calls and send numerous e-mails to learn how the project was progressing. Finally, after many frustrating weeks she realized there was a cultural disconnect—*yes* means one thing for Americans and another for their Indian colleagues. For them, *yes* means "I heard you," while it means "I'll get it done" to an American.

Saying *No*. Barbara, a virtual leader at a global technology IPO, offered this story:

> "Part of our due diligence was to create a marketing plan to support our business strategy for different cultures. When I did a combination of in-person and virtual interviews with folks in the Asia/Pacific region, I found out that in many oriental cultures there simply isn't a word for *no*. The market research firm that designed a survey had yes/no answers, and we didn't realize that the resulting data was skewed. Everyone answered 'yes' and it took us a while to realize that."

Barbara continued with an interesting experience that she had in Tokyo:

> "At a meeting with senior executives, my chair was placed in the middle of the room—there was no table—with all the other chairs set in a half-moon around me. I sat there with all eyes on me, feeling interrogated, but from their perspective I was given a place of honor. The translator answered my questions 'yes,' but I could see them shake their heads 'no.' Their body language also said 'no.' It hadn't occurred to me that they were saying yes but not meaning it until I saw it with my own eyes. At that point we redid the survey using only multiple-choice questions. If I hadn't gone to Singapore and Tokyo, I wouldn't have noticed this cultural disconnect.
>
> "I learned that on virtual teams you must be very explicit in your communications and constantly hold daily calls at certain times. If we don't do that, productivity levels off. I pick a specific issue or question and then ask everyone to weigh in. I'm a big believer in using a 1 to 5 scale to pinpoint what I'm trying to find out. I keep it simple, with 5 [being] the best. I say, 'How is [fill in the blank]? Is it more like a 4 or 5, or just a 1 or 2?'"

"Okay, We Got It." Arlene, a client who works from a home office in Connecticut managing a virtual team for a pharmaceutical giant, told me the following story:

"My number-one issue when I communicate with my virtual team members is understanding their accents on the phone. I deal with people from China, South Africa, India, and Costa Rica, and I often can't understand what they say, and sometimes it's worse with tech teams. There are additional issues that come up with our developers in India. When they first joined my team I would lay out deadlines and describe specs, and no matter what I said they would say, 'Okay, we got it,' and 'Yes, we're okay,' but things were not okay and they weren't delivered on time. It didn't take me long to realize that they said 'okay' instead of asking questions.

"So I kept very detailed notes of what I wanted to accomplish on each call, and for important points I asked them to repeat back what I said. It went like this: I would say, 'I need to make sure you deliver [this expected result or product] by [date].' After giving them a few seconds to think it over I would then say, 'What did I just ask for?' Someone would shoot back, 'ABC,' and I would then say, 'No, it's XYZ.' We went back and forth until I was satisfied that what I conveyed was understood and would be acted on in a timely manner. But it didn't stop there. I then followed up the phone call with an e-mail. All this took a lot longer than I was used to, but I got the results I wanted."

What Can You Take Away from These Situations?

As a virtual manager you may have faced similar issues and have put in place similar solutions, which are based on common sense and respect for others. Although the specifics of these three situations differ and the virtual managers come from different industries, they all shared the need to understand and to be understood by others. Keeping the communication clean so that things don't get lost in translation is one of your key responsibilities, especially when business English is the "part-time" language of many team members. The three managers adapted to the cultural cues, and I am confident that by following their suggestions, you will have the same success with your team:

1. Keep detailed notes of what you need accomplished on calls so that you are clear at all times on how the virtual meeting is progressing.

2. Conduct frequent check-ins where everyone voices an opinion.

3. When you ask a question, use a Likert scale of 1 to 5 with specific, explicit choices (strongly disagree, disagree, neither agree nor disagree, agree, or strongly agree). Ask open-ended questions; don't provide informative answers.

4. Ask team members to repeat what you said to ensure understanding.

5. Follow up with phone calls and e-mails, and be as explicit as possible.

What Do I Do if They Don't Speak My Language?

Being foreign-born, I am always sensitive to how I speak, especially when interacting with people from other cultures. In these circumstances, I keep an open mind, sharpen my "people antenna" to get a better read of the situation, and ask questions. I am always willing to learn about other cultures, and I make an effort to understand what someone else's language means.

Here are some suggestions for what to do when people don't speak your language.

If You Are the Non-native Speaker

➤ Appreciate that your strong accent, for example, may make it difficult for others to understand you. You can say something like, "I know that I have a strong accent. Please do not hesitate to interrupt me whenever something is unclear to you, or ask me to repeat what I said more slowly."

If You Are the Native Speaker

➤ Be aware that you may slip into colloquialisms, talk very fast, mumble, or speak with a regional accent, all of which hinder a non-native speaker's comprehension. Therefore, it is helpful to speak slowly and say up front, "If necessary, please stop me and ask me to repeat something or ask for a further explanation."

➤ Keep in mind the dangers of using slang, particularly with people whose English is their part-time language because they may not always understand the meaning behind the expression. For example, Americans often use the term *slam dunk* without realizing that even fluent speakers of English from other cultures are not aware of its meaning as a "sure thing."

Additional Tips

➤ Cue your verbal and nonverbal behaviors to your audience.

➤ Repeat! Yes, repeat important ideas and explain the concept with different words.

➤ Check comprehension by asking colleagues to repeat their understanding of the material back to you. Do not assume your audience understands what you say. Don't just ask, "Do you understand what I mean?" Ask them to explain what they heard, in their own words.

➤ Pause more frequently.

➤ When there is a silence, wait. Do not jump in to fill the silence. The other person is probably just translating your words.

➤ Do not equate poor grammar and mispronunciation with lack of intelligence; it is usually a sign of second-language use.

➤ On long conference calls, take more frequent breaks. Second-language comprehension can be exhausting.

➤ Divide your presentation into small modules with frequent checkpoints so that listeners don't fall behind.

➤ E-mail team members summaries of your verbal presentation.

The Five Clusters That Comprise All Cross-Cultural Interactions

Given that people from different cultures view the world and events through their own cultural lens (just see how many different definitions of *virtual team* your team members would come up with if asked), understanding cultural nuances is an overriding consideration. Since virtual teams, by definition, comprise individuals from different locations, there is a good chance that your team will also have people from a variety of cultures. Although it is tempting to overlook these differences, by doing so you run the risk of causing needless friction that can impact team performance.

My consulting practice has spanned various industries and locales, and over the years engagements have taken me all over the world. I realized that regardless of how a team was organized or the nature of its mission, themes emerged around how team members interact. That is, within every culture certain factors consistently appear when people work together. For clarity and consistency, I have grouped these factors into what I call clusters (five in all) that comprise cross-cultural interactions. Team members are usually selected because of their technical skills, without considering how cultural backgrounds may affect team interactions. And yet, as you saw in Chapter 6, technical skills alone will not get deliverables out the door if miscommunications and perceived slights occur that can derail efforts. By examining these clusters, you will understand the specific aspects of culture that can lead to these difficulties.

The five clusters are:

1. Mindset
2. Persona
3. Orientation
4. Structure
5. Process

Within each cluster, think about the cultural styles represented on your team, and the preferences individuals show, which are derived from their culture of origin. Note that most behaviors fall along a continuum, and there is no right or wrong.

In my experience, managers produce high-performing teams when they consider the unique cultural perspectives of team members. Use this awareness of how culture impacts behavior across the five clusters to encourage appropriate team interactions. Ask yourself how you can build on differences to pull individuals together into a successful team. Or, as I like to say, how can you combine these wonderful ingredients to make a great Pepper Pot Soup?

Cluster 1: Mindset (the "What")

> "The biggest difference between American and Asian cultures is collaboration. It wasn't until I worked on a post-merger implementation with my Asian counterparts that I came up against their culture. They are very collaborative and they work to complete what the boss wants. I don't like to assign tasks, I like my team to speak up and ask questions. I don't care if we disagree—that energizes me. But I had to initiate discussions and challenge the process because they wouldn't challenge someone more senior."
>
> —VT LEADER, INSURANCE COMPANY

Mindset refers to our underlying assumptions, beliefs, and attitudes about the world; it's how we make sense of what our senses take in, and is heavily influenced by the culture around us. Mindset guides our thinking process and behavior, and becomes ingrained through repetition, which reinforces our initial responses.

Mindset encompasses the following factors:

> *Global vs. Local Perspective.* What lens do you use to view the world? Do you have a short-focus or a wide-angle lens? Some people look at their immediate surroundings, favoring close colleagues and focusing on what's good for their immediate group. Others take a broader approach and look beyond their own comfort zone to include various perspectives.

> *Collaborative vs. Competitive.* Think about your attitude and underlying assumptions when interacting with other people. Do you approach things in a more participative way, seeking input from others, or do you have "sharp elbows" when advocating strongly for your own point of view?

> *Consultative vs. Decisive.* While a preference for collaborating or competing speaks to our attitudes, a decisive or consultative approach directly relates to the process of how we make decisions and go about solving problems. Do you consult others and strive for consensus, or do you "decide and announce" a plan, without input from others?

> *Task-Oriented vs. Relationship-Oriented.* Which comes first, the relationship or the task? Do you focus on developing the relationship before conducting business, or do you go straight to the issues at hand without building the relationships that make success possible?

Cluster 2: Persona (the "Who")

> "I often travel to Santo Domingo on business. On my first trip, I asked a question and I would get an answer that had no basis in reality. For example, if I asked, 'How long does it take to get from A to B?' I would be told ten minutes, but it was really an hour away. Everything was ten minutes because no one wanted any negativity; nothing was too hard to do, nothing was too far away. So I started asking questions in a more general way, like, 'If you were going to [this place], how long would it take to get there?' or 'When would you leave here to get to [that place]?' The trick was *not* to ask the question as if I was considering going there myself. Then I would get the truth."
>
> —BEVERAGE COMPANY EXECUTIVE

What face do you put forward when communicating? Persona is the way we present ourselves to the world and how we approach others. It is a set of behaviors that allows us to interact with someone in a culturally appropriate way. These behaviors are typically based on deeply rooted cultural norms that have shaped us from childhood. Every culture has an expected dynamic that people from that culture prefer when interacting.

Here are the key behaviors associated with Persona:

> ➤ *Holding Opinions to Oneself vs. Voicing Opinions.* Do individuals keep things to themselves or do they voice their thoughts and concerns? The answer to this question may reflect people's personal styles as well as cultural biases. Either people have a willingness to share an opinion and hash out an issue, or they prefer to keep their thoughts private and not risk losing face.

> ➤ *Agreeable vs. Willing to Disagree.* During discussions, do you go along with what people say, even though you may not concur, or are you willing to openly disagree?

> ➤ *Public or Private.* Do individuals share details about their personal life or family, or are they more reticent?

> ➤ *Question Authority or Acquiesce.* How does one act when dealing with someone in a superior position? What face do you

show? Are you willing to respectfully question authority or do you accept an authority figure's word and think, "That's the way it is"?

Cluster 3: Orientation (the "When")

"I allotted thirty minutes for a gentleman from Pakistan to explain a pilot program during a conference. He spoke eloquently, but unfortunately he was extremely long-winded and spent a great deal of time thanking different people, which took time away from the core content. My boss told me to move his presentation along, so I had to ask him to wrap it up. I passed him a note which said, PLEASE—ONLY FIVE MORE MINUTES, I'M SORRY. [Afterward] I had to save face and apologize, saying that I didn't schedule enough time for his presentation. It was an uncomfortable situation, with a lot of tension. The Canadians, Americans, and Brits felt he was wasting time and they were really annoyed. It's still the 'Western way is the better way' sentiment."

—HR EXECUTIVE, INTERNATIONAL RESCUE ORGANIZATION

Orientation is about the way that you view time and value its use. Cultural frameworks determine our view of the nature of time and, therefore, our choices around how we spend it.

Here are key components to evaluate within Orientation:

> *Present or Future.* Do you think about what's happening right now or what's happening in the future? In addition, is your focus on the short term or long term?

> *Limited or Plentiful.* The issue here is related to time as a commodity. If we view each moment as unique and scarce, then time is considered to be a limited commodity that must be maximized (multitasking, anyone?). If time is renewable, like the cyclical processes of nature, then it will always be there in large quantities.

> *Slow or Fast Pace.* This issue deals with activity as it relates to time. If time is a limited commodity, then you'll function at a faster pace, packing more activities and initiatives into your waking hours. However, cultures that take a long view of time typically function at a slower pace and are frequently

characterized as patient; it is more important to participate in a process than to meet deadlines or to be punctual. Think of it as the difference between packing twenty-five hours of activities into a twenty-four-hour day and *engaging* in several hours' worth of activities in the same twenty-four-hour period.

Cluster 4: Structure (the "How to Organize")

"When my company was bought by a world leader, I was put on a team that looked at new markets, and we had Koreans and Americans gathering data. One guy, an American from the Northeast, kept asking his Korean contact for some information, to no avail. Finally, he complained directly to a higher-level Korean manager and caused a major rift because he didn't realize that Koreans operate in a hierarchy. The higher-level Korean manager and Korean team members were offended. We were from a small company where the only thing that mattered was getting things done. You have to learn to adjust, and I did."

—VT MEMBER, ELECTRONICS GIANT

Structure is the approach to order and the degree of flexibility around that order. Cultures order their world according to expectations, norms, and roles. A society can be more tolerant or less tolerant of deviation, uncertainty, and disorder; its structure mirrors the extent of that tolerance.

Here are the key behavioral components to evaluate within Structure:

> *Precise vs. Loose.* Does your culture take a literal view of how order is approached? If so, there will be greater structure, with a precise order imposed from the top and highly detailed rules of behavior. At the other end of the continuum is loose structure, with fewer rules about social behavior.

> *Hierarchical vs. Entrepreneurial.* Is power centralized, hierarchical, and tightly defined, or is the environment more entrepreneurial and not as defined? Business organizations, among others, are structured around how centralized and hierarchical the power structure is, and how tightly defined and controlled responsibilities are within an organization.

Entrepreneurial businesses or cultures, by comparison, operate in an environment where the power structure is not as defined. Here, individuals are empowered to some degree, and power-sharing arrangements are common.

> ➤ *Formal vs. Informal.* Do people address each other formally or informally? Are titles very important or nonexistent? It is important to know answers to these questions when we do business with other cultures to avoid needless friction. Some cultures place a lot of emphasis on the formality of the interaction, while in other cultures title and status are not as important. A culture that values formality attaches significance to tradition, rules and rank, status and power, while informal cultures have a casual attitude and value more egalitarian organizations with smaller differences in status and power.

Cluster 5: Process (the "How to Do It")

"When I started this job we had fifty to sixty people: thirty-five in Beijing, the rest in Germany, U.K., Australia, Canada, and the U.S. I had a big task of getting them to collaborate, although I didn't speak any other language but English. The group in Beijing was between [the ages of] 25 to 35. The rest of the people in the organization had been there longer and survived several downturns. They were in their fifties and felt that they knew it all. We had cultural clashes between the young Chinese, who were waiting for instructions, and experienced Americans/Europeans, who wanted to get the objectives and be left alone. So I hired a cultural expert and conducted cultural sensitivity training. It really helped, but the real coming together for the team was our sailing trip. One team member had a giant sailboat and took us all for a sail. Some Chinese teammates were never on a boat before, so they were happy to try something new. It was a great bonding experience—coming together as a team—and performance increased afterward. To this day, people still talk about this sailing experience. Maybe next time I'll take them on a boat race."

—VT LEADER, BIOCHEMICAL COMPANY

Process is how we get things done. There are multiple stages with people working together to transform ideas into actions to achieve specific goals. Process is the approach one takes in pursuit of these goals.

Here are key descriptors within Process:

> *Planning Ahead vs. Just-in-Time.* What is the value your culture places on planning, from an idea's inception through execution to fruition? Is the culture considered methodical, where it is customary to plan ahead, with clearly defined steps of a process? Or is it a just-in-time culture, where things are usually dealt with as needed, when they come up, instead of planned for with what-if scenarios?

> *Linear vs. Fluid Thinking.* How are projects planned, problems solved, and critical components of a deliverable realized? Societies that place a heavy emphasis on tradition and order will follow the tried-and-true process, whereas societies that encourage the new will gravitate toward a more fluid approach that explores new ways of achieving results.

> *General vs. Detail.* People with a general outlook bring a big-picture perspective to an entire process, while people with a detailed approach look at individual components and a situation's specifics.

Integrating the Five Cultural Clusters into Your Business Etiquette

Now that you've examined these five cultural clusters, think about your own team. It is helpful to understand how these clusters relate to a wide array of constituencies—peers, direct reports, executives, clients, and vendors, among others. Recognizing how someone's cultural values might influence behavior is the first step in building CCC skills. Figure 7-3 presents an exercise you can use to gain a deeper perspective on your team's cultural differences. I am confident your recipe for Pepper Pot Soup will score points with every stakeholder.

Figure 7-3. Five cultural clusters and their components.

Within each **cluster** (column 1), which **component** (column 2) is currently your team's **biggest challenge** (column 3)? What **actions** or further steps can you take in this world of diminished cues (column 4)?

Cluster	Components	My Team's Biggest Challenge	Future Steps for My Team
MINDSET **"The What"**	• Global vs. Local Perspective • Collaborative vs. Competitive • Task-Oriented vs. Relationship-Oriented		
PERSONA **"The Who"**	• Holding Opinions to Oneself vs. Voicing Opinions • Agreeable vs. Willing to Disagree • Public or Private • Question Authority or Acquiesce		
ORIENTATION **"The When"**	• Present or Future • Limited or Plentiful • Slow or Fast Pace		
STRUCTURE **"The How to Organize"**	• Precise vs. Loose • Hierarchical vs. Entrepreneurial • Formal vs. Informal		
PROCESS **"The How to Do It"**	• Planning Ahead vs. Just-In-Time (JIT) • Linear vs. Fluid Thinking • General vs. Detail		

Five Effective Strategies for Cross-Cultural Interactions

You can L E A R N to improve your daily interactions by incorporating the strategies behind this acronym into your CCC.

Listen

Effectively Communicate

Avoid Ambiguity

Respect Differences

No Judgment

Strategy 1: Listen

Active listening is the single most useful way to overcome barriers to effective communication. We listen for meaning by checking back with the speaker to ensure that we have accurately heard and understood what was said. Communicating across cultures adds another layer to the "noise" that is present, which makes it critical to add that extra step of checking back. Active listening is the key to avoiding misinterpretations. For example, people from different cultures may use the same word in different ways (as we've already seen), so repeating what you think you heard and asking if that's what the speaker intended confirms your understanding of the word's meaning.

Learn to get beyond the distractions that may interfere with properly hearing your speaker, such as accents, limited vocabulary, and lack of nuance or thorough understanding of a language. Be attuned to the speaker's cultural background and communication style.

Beyond active listening, you can tone down your language, avoiding harsh and/or difficult words as well as adjusting the timing and speed of your speech. Incorporate the following techniques into your everyday communication:

> ➤ Listen without considering what you will say next. Take the time to listen rather than try to guess what's being said. Avoid thinking ahead.

➤ Ask questions to ensure that you accurately understand the message being conveyed.

➤ Paraphrase back to the speaker to clarify understanding.

➤ Avoid multitasking when listening to virtual team members.

➤ Consider the speaker's background when evaluating the message, and be aware of and suspend assumptions based on your own cultural interpretations.

➤ Use a headset if possible, to keep your hands free so that you can take notes to verify the important points of the conversation and the action items that need attention with your colleagues.

Strategy 2: Effectively Communicate

Aim to keep the communication lines open and transparent so that when conflicts arise—and they will—a resolution is found quickly. Here is a helpful four-step technique to keep the cultural communication lines open:

1. Respond with appropriate words that will not inflame a situation, when you sense difficulty.
2. Deliver balanced feedback.
3. Build on an idea.
4. Give credit/positive reinforcement.

For examples of situations when you might use each of the four techniques and what to say, see Figure 7-4.

Since virtual teams rely heavily on voice communications, they need to compensate for the lack of visual cues. Regarding teleconferences, here are some good practices to follow:

➤ If the conversation appears to be coming to a close, conclude with a transition or sum-up statement. For example, "So you are saying that . . ."

➤ Allow the other person to complete his thoughts. Avoid dominating the conversation, even if you feel you have a lot to say.

> ➤ If the other person sounds bored and uninterested, change the subject and/or direction of the conversation. Keep the other person involved by asking questions, and even asking where the person would like the conversation to go.

Figure 7-4. CCC technique: respond, give feedback, improve ideas, give credit.

When to Respond:	What to Say:
• If you have an impulse to disagree with, reject, or ignore what someone has said.	• Ask/e-mail for confirmation. *"In other words, Tom, you're saying that . . ."* or *"Let me see if I understand you, Tom . . ."*
• If you don't understand what or why something was said.	• Ask/e-mail for clarification first; then ask for confirmation. *"I'm not sure I understand. Could you say more about . . . ?"* or *"Why is that?"* or *"Oh?"*

When to Give Balanced Feedback:	What to Say:
• To influence another or when you have concerns about someone's work or idea.	• Itemize the merits and faults in the correct order, making them specific and task related. • Always express faults as concerns, not criticisms! *"Your implementation plan for a 256-slice machine is ambitious, and I'm concerned that we don't have the resources to write the software code as quickly as you need it."*
• When you see a way to overcome the concerns you've itemized.	• Offer suggestions that retain the merits and eliminate the faults. *"In view of this, I think it would be better to perfect the software before we commit to showing real images for the next sales cycle."*
• To continue the conversation *after* you've offered your suggestions.	• Invite further comments. *"What do you think about that?"* or *"Do you have any other suggestions?"*

When to Build on an Idea:	What to Say:
• When you see a way to improve someone's idea or suggestion.	• Indicate the connection between the person's idea and what you'll say. *"What you said makes me think that . . ."* or *"Not only that, but it would also make sense to . . ."* • Then, mention an additional benefit or advantage, and/or suggest a modification. *"If we could put 'X system' in place, then production could start within a month on the new model."*

• If you've modified the person's idea.	• Check to be sure you haven't distorted what the person was originally trying to accomplish. *"What do you think?"* or *"Would that still accomplish what you wanted?"*

When to Give Credit/Positive Reinforcement:	**What to Say:**
• To increase the likelihood of a behavior recurring or to compliment someone whose behavior exceeds expectations.	• Make a general reference to what you're crediting. *"Nice work, Tom. I like your ideas on image resolution."* • Provide a specific example of the idea or task being credited. *"I particularly liked the simplicity of what you're suggesting."* • If appropriate, mention the qualities that led to the success. *"It took a lot of creative thinking to come up with that one."* • Indicate the benefits. *"It sure will help marketing generate interest in our newest models."*

Strategy 3: Avoid Ambiguity

Awareness of culturally derived differences in behavior and communication decreases ambiguity. The ability to avoid ambiguity is directly tied to active listening skills. Avoiding or tolerating ambiguity doesn't necessarily mean that you deliberately avoid these types of situations. You want to be able to react to new, different, and potentially unpredictable situations, but you also want to avoid the uneasiness in such situations that can lead to frustration and hinder your ability to communicate. The greater your knowledge about another culture the less ambiguous it becomes, and when someone behaves accordingly you won't be surprised and uncertain.

These suggestions can help build a virtual environment that avoids ambiguity:

➤ Create a safe, friendly environment that encourages participation.

➤ Share information about team members' cultural backgrounds.

➤ Be careful with humor. It can be easily misunderstood, or even considered offensive in many cultures. In most cases, it is best to just avoid making jokes.

➤ Recognize your own assumptions and prejudgments, which may be clouded by cultural backgrounds, past experiences, and a subconscious bias.

➤ Encourage participation in conference calls so that questions are brought up.

➤ Build in feedback loops (e.g., asking questions, paraphrasing what someone says, asking someone to repeat a statement) to ensure clarity.

Strategy 4: Respect Differences

Effective CCC can be difficult if you have trouble showing respect for another person's differences. Just as you want to be respected for different characteristics that you may bring to a group, others do as well. Attitude is everything, and you can encourage team members to think of their differences as the spice that lends interest to your Pepper Pot Soup.

While different cultures vary in how they show respect (e.g., the bow is customary in Japan), following these general rules should lead to positive results:

➤ Make it your business to learn at least one fact about every team member's culture.

➤ Acknowledge cultural differences and remind teammates to respect them.

➤ Be professional; make it a point to assume a clear and welcoming tone when you communicate by phone.

➤ Be punctual when meeting someone new from an unfamiliar culture.

➤ Do not overgeneralize or attribute characteristics of a given culture to individuals; in other words, refrain from stereotyping, even when others around you do it.

➤ Use optimistic, positive terms in your written or oral communication.

➤ Find every opportunity to acknowledge others.

➤ Demonstrate flexibility. Be open to discussing other options. If you find that you and the person with whom you are speaking want different things, try to find a middle ground and compromise. Being rigid and too tied to your way of doing things could set back your progress.

➤ Learn to use the words for "please" and "thank you" in the individual's native tongue. Although no one expects you to master a slew of foreign languages, this simple gesture is appreciated.

➤ Watch or read the news from your team members' countries of origin. Discuss cultural topics to better understand different viewpoints (although it may be best to avoid political issues).

➤ Become aware of the traditional festivals of your virtual team members' countries. They may genuinely appreciate an e-mail or IM greeting on those days.

➤ Use social networks to learn more about your virtual coworkers.

➤ Respect different time zones when scheduling virtual meetings. Work toward sharing this responsibility so that everyone's availability and time preferences are honored equally.

Practice Active Communication in a Virtual Environment: Five Steps to Manage Differences

Look at these situations, some of which you may have experienced firsthand. The proposed solutions are taken from various client sessions where we brainstormed how best to respond to the issues and situations stated.

Situation:	Appropriate Action:
You don't have enough information to respond to a disagreement through feedback or alternatives.	1. **Ask for clarification** to get a better understanding of the other person's needs or concerns. *"I'm not sure how you propose to get this done in six weeks. Could you walk me through your plan?"*
You understand someone's needs and concerns and are willing to consider alternatives.	2. **Suggest and/or ask for alternatives.** This may bring clarification and confirmation or lead to an opportunity for giving balanced feedback or building on an idea. *"I'm willing to look at other suppliers that are within our cost guidelines, but what will you do to ensure quality control?"*
You are still uncertain about what someone wants, and you want to continue the discussion.	3. **State what's important to you, and check what's important to the other person.** *"What matters to me is getting clean images quickly at a reasonable cost. If I understand you correctly, you can guarantee the quality of the images, but the cost is prohibitive."*
You are still unable to identify alternatives and want to probe further.	4. **Temporarily remove restrictions.** This may bring clarification and confirmation, or lead to an opportunity for balanced feedback or idea building, or additional alternatives. *"If there weren't any restrictions, Brenda, what would you like to do?"*
You clearly understand someone's needs and concerns and have spent sufficient time trying to identify alternatives.	5. **End discussion (acknowledging the other person's views and feelings), and state your decision.** *"Raj, I understand why you want marketing to promote this new application, but it will come back to haunt us if we can't deliver it. I can't go along with what you are proposing to management."*

Strategy 5: No Judgment

Respecting others means suspending judgment. Try this simple technique: Instead of jumping to conclusions consider that your cultural lens may distort the truth. Consider several alternative possibilities and use this three-part evaluation approach:

1. Describe (e.g., "Nat joins the call late every Monday").

2. Interpret (e.g., "Nat doesn't care about the job").

3. Evaluate (e.g., "I'll give Nat the less desirable projects").

Now, consider the same evaluation approach with the addition of one more step in which you consider several options. This step is the one that many people skip, leading them to erroneous and often biased conclusions.

Describe. The situation that is causing concern is that "Nat joins the call late every Monday." This time, before you make an assumption, consider several reasons for his tardy behavior. For example:

➤ He has familial obligations every Monday morning.

➤ His start-of-week meeting with his boss always runs late.

➤ He oversleeps after the weekend.

➤ He doesn't care about the job.

Interpret. Once you've formulated several hypotheses for Nat's behavior, you are ready to make your interpretation. "Nat's tardiness could be due to a factor that may be out of his control."

Evaluate. "I will talk to Nat about his tardiness and learn more about why it's happening."

Additional Tips for Working Across Cultures

➤ Don't assume that other people think/behave the way you do.

➤ Accept the possibility that whatever occurred could be an anomaly caused by any number of circumstances (e.g., someone having a bad day or dealing with personal issues).

➤ Be aware of your personal biases (i.e., increase your self-awareness). Treat people as individuals and not as generalized stereotypes.

➤ Remain positive. Don't always assume the worst/negative outcome.

➤ Avoid blaming others.

➤ Take the time to reflect before saying/doing something that you may regret.

➤ Avoid making comments such as, "You don't understand" or "What's your problem?" These kinds of remarks may cause the other party to respond defensively.

➤ Use descriptive and nonevaluative language when communicating with others.

➤ Refrain from seeing things at the extremes (e.g., black/white, right/wrong) since there are many shades of gray.

➤ Be mindful of terms people use to explain themselves and the world around them, because certain terms have different meanings across cultures.

⌐ − −CASE STUDY

They Moved Me to . . . a Storage Room

As we near the end of this chapter I would like to share one last client story. Brigit was a British national (transferred to Japan) who managed a joint U.K.–Japanese project. The team was charged with building an interface for a large customer database. Brigit's boss appreciated her probing style, which usually got right to the heart of an issue. When deadlines started to slip she made him, as well as her Japanese team members, aware of the situation and shared key points with all. Although her boss appreciated this honest assessment her Japanese colleagues did not share his point of view. They were embarrassed because she violated their norms for 1) showing respect to someone at a more senior level and 2) uncovering and discussing problems.

"They moved me to an office that was in reality a storage room," she told me. "There I was, far removed from the people and information that I needed to keep tabs on how the project was going. My colleagues only spoke to me when I was absolutely needed. It was clear to me that in Japan coworkers keep their opinions to themselves. They don't question authority, they just want to work in a harmonious place. They probably would have responded better if I had pointed out the problems indirectly. I should have said, 'What would happen if shipping charges would not calculate properly?' even though this was exactly what was happening and I knew that it was."

When I was hired to coach Brigit she told me flat out that "perception is reality" and said that she understood that only she could repair her reputation. Thoughtful and highly motivated to develop better work relationships, she used the L E A R N strategies with her team. When the project ended, several Japanese colleagues surprised her with a lavish good-bye banquet before she returned to London—a true testament to what anyone can achieve by focusing on these commonsense tools.

Driving Along the Cross-Cultural Highway

In this chapter, you read comments by virtual managers who have earned their global driver's license. Today, even if you manage locally, you deal with multicultural elements and work across diverse CCC styles. To work effectively in this environment you need to understand people if you hope to influence and motivate them to achieve business results. You need to become a *manager of cultures*.

Whether local or global, look at the landscape beyond the horizon, recognizing that events at one location impact another. I call this type of visionary leadership Vista-Leadership (more about this concept in Chapter 8). It requires advanced understanding, visioning, and extreme openness to how people interact in different cultures. As so beautifully put by a client who led a global team at a health care solutions company, "When it comes to becoming a manager of cultures, you need to know that you don't know. There are so many unknowns and you have to manage and look for them; people don't speak exactly what they mean. They maintain distance, and when you are a global manager who is not from their [location], you need to understand them."

To gain clarity on your team's cross-cultural interactions, reflect once again on the five Cultural Clusters. Use them to assess your team members, and then complete the Virtual Roadmap exercise at the end of the chapter. It is designed to help you integrate the L E A R N strategies that will best address the specific challenges within your team, as well as further expand your team's thinking about cross-cultural communication, adaptation, and integration.

YOUR VIRTUAL ROADMAP TO CROSS-CULTURAL COMMUNICATION

Step 1. Populate each column of this team grid with key information about each team member.

MAP YOUR TEAM GRID

Team Member	Cultural Background	Key CCC Challenge (refer to the Cultural Clusters and choose the component that presents the greatest challenge for that individual)	L E A R N (strategy to improve your interaction)

Step 2. When you have completed this team grid, ask yourself three key questions:

1. How can I engage my team to effectively communicate across cultures?
2. What strengths and areas for improvement exist on my team?
3. How can I build greater interaction and help members gain greater appreciation of each other?

You now have all the information you need to create what I call a Third Culture team. Remember that every individual brings a unique point of view to a shared experience. Even though facts may stand on their own, our perspectives differ. So what is there to do?

Let's Do It Our Way: The Third Culture

Every culture is internalized by its people, ingrained in the "software of their minds." Your team may contain an American way, a Chinese way, a German way, a "you fill in the blanks" way. Your challenge is to lead these individuals to adaptation and integration.

Here's an activity I do with my clients that brings about a "meeting of the minds." We create what I call the Third Culture, meaning that things don't have to be your way or my way; we can come up with a *third way* by establishing our group culture. I ask team members to arrange themselves in groups of mixed cultures to discuss the following:

- Briefly describe our group culture.
- What aspects of our culture support performance?
- What aspects of our culture hinder performance?
- Where does our culture need to be tomorrow?
- What gaps exist and how can we bridge those gaps?
- What cultural values must we share to succeed as a team?

Based on their answers, participants then have to codify a Third Culture for their team. But first, I ask: *What cultural barriers might get in the way of your team's Third Culture?* Often mentioned are language differences, cultural bias, psychological distance, lack of common goals, or team members' inability to adapt to new ways of doing things. We then visually list (write down) these items and discuss ways to overcome them. We conclude with a list of best practices to accelerate team performance and end the session with a tangible code of conduct for participants to take with them on their virtual journey.

CHAPTER 8

Virtual Teams and the Future

What will virtual teams look like in the future? With the workplace undergoing change at the speed of light, we may have to consult science fiction for a possible answer. Will colleagues sit in their offices in front of incredibly complex machines? Or will we become officeless human beings, performing our jobs while wearing personal networks? I have had multiple discussions about the "death" of the workplace and the "birth" of the virtual space, and you may have as well.

Technology is so embedded in the workplace that we take its marvels for granted, yet the human adjustment is still in a state of flux. This is the reality you face, and leading successfully requires a new set of skills in light of voluminous data, rapid information flow, and intense collaboration. We are all wired and connected, yet many people feel so disconnected. Given the circumstances, I wonder how we will maintain that most basic human need for interaction, communication, and connection.

Connection is a common denominator across the human experience, and it goes beyond time and space, transcending all boundaries. This book began with the first leg of your journey to create this human connection across your team, and subsequent chapters explored ways to Set Up, Follow Through (through implementation and performance), and Refresh your team. Now, let's conclude with a look into the future of virtual teams.

Throughout this book I introduced a number of principles, tools, and examples to guide your journey down the virtual highway. To master the virtual equation and make these elements work together, you have to become the connector. In fact, your greatest role as a manager is to link the various parts of your team to accomplish the goals that led to its formation in the first place. You may need to shift gears, perform team tune-ups, realign, and refuel your team's energy along the way.

Look at how quickly our world is transforming. Technologies and industries unheard of just fifteen years ago are well integrated into our lives, and some of the most valuable companies in the world today did not even exist back then. The Internet opens up a vast wealth of information that we have incorporated into daily existence. It is difficult to keep up with all the new developments in technology, much less understand their implications. It's as if we are driving 200 miles (321.87 kilometers) an hour and only look at the rearview mirror. But don't get too comfortable with today's world—because it's changing as you read these words.

Moving from Agent of Change to Agent of Connection

Because of the complexity of our modern world, dramatic as well as incremental changes will occur, and many of them will be beyond your control. In the not-too-distant past, effective leaders were considered Agents of Change, with sole responsibility for getting their teams to rise to organizational challenges. That no longer works, as no one person, regardless how talented and hardworking, is capable of mastering all that is required of business leadership today.

Leadership issues always surface in my consulting and coaching engagements. Over the years, working internally in organizations and as an external practitioner, I have facilitated discussions about what makes one leader more successful than another and worked with executives to sharpen their capabilities in this area. At the beginning of my career the concept of "managing change" was at the core of these sessions. However, about a dozen years ago I began shifting my focus from viewing the leader as an Agent of Change to what I have come to call an Agent of Connection.

Here is what led to this mind shift: I was called in by a large financial services firm to help facilitate the rollout of a complex, large-scale IT project. After working with managers from various locations for several weeks, I noticed that managers who oversaw successful launches were those who collaborated with individuals outside their own span of control. It wasn't a matter of understanding what needed to be "changed" and trying to manage that change; their success was directly related to how well they connected with others and their willingness to trust their own team to solve issues. I saw clearly that one person could not do it all. Leadership itself was changing.

Leadership in the virtual workplace has reflected the paradigm shift that has occurred, bringing a new order of business relationships and a new definition for the role of the leader. The very nature of a dispersed team means that virtual leaders like you can no longer successfully manage through command-and-control techniques. Leadership takes confidence in your team and the tenacity to integrate people, despite time and space constraints. Your team members may be out of sight, but they can't be out of mind.

And so a different kind of leadership is emerging, which focuses on connection and collaboration and encourages people to rise above their differences and connect at the human level. At its core, this leadership is rooted in the human element and reflects an increased level of trust and transparency. This updated role as the Agent of Connection is your most important role as a virtual leader.

I developed a set of leadership behaviors that I call GlobaLeadership (GL). The letter *L* is shared by the words because leadership is both shared and global in a dispersed team environment. As one of my favorite clients, who managed a virtual team for a medical device manufacturer, has said: "It doesn't matter whether or not you are a global manager, and it isn't important if you don't have a global assignment—you are global."

Seven GlobaLeadership Dimensions

Picture yourself at the hub of a wide network of connections that enables you to achieve competitive advantage. You, the Agent of Connection, are at the center of this GL model, surrounded by the seven dimensions that are critical for effective virtual team leadership. These dimensions are:

1. Vista-Leadership

2. Innova-Leadership

3. Adapta-Leadership

4. Diversa-Leadership

5. Communi-Leadership

6. Collabo-Leadership

7. Edu-Leadership

Each dimension represents a necessary skill in organizational leadership; however, rarely does one single individual excel at both a core business function and all seven dimensions. For this reason, I consider the true virtual leader an Agent of Connection, because the leader is the one who links individual team members who have complementary strengths in one or more of these critical dimensions. This leader assesses the competitive landscape, determines which dimensions are essential for success, and then orchestrates the efforts of a strong team that contains these qualities. Figure 8-1 describes the seven dimensions of leadership.

Figure 8-1. The seven dimensions of leadership.

Dimension of Leadership	Description
Vista-Leadership	Vista-Leadership enables leaders to envision the future business environment while being grounded, but not stuck, in the present. A leader who practices Vista-Leadership has a wide horizon, distills potential possibilities from known elements, and is comfortable with the unfamiliar. Employing Vista-Leadership skills means navigating at 30,000 feet

and having the widest possible viewpoint imaginable. When leaders master this leadership dimension, then inspiration and breakthrough thinking fuel their team's ability to see past clutter and operationalize the company's vision, to make sound business decisions with the entire organization/landscape in mind.

Innova-Leadership	Innova-Leadership is about seeking new ways to achieve competitive advantage by drawing on and expanding resources. To put clever ideas into action, leaders must be confident working with the unknown, using their imagination and encouraging others to be creative—even if it causes disorder. In fact, leaders with strong Innova-Leadership skills understand that stable systems destabilize when they are ready to advance to a higher level, and therefore they actively create disruption to further the organization's advancement. When applying Innova-Leadership to their organization, leaders can reshape their team's culture and structure.
Adapta-Leadership	Adapta-Leadership enables leaders to move in any direction at any time in any situation as they learn from their experiences in the moment and adapt accordingly. When leading change, leaders maintain a positive attitude and successfully address issues around resistance. They succeed at integrating disparate forces to achieve business results and are adept at working through nonlinear and disruptive phases and processes. In this era of accelerating change, foresight is necessary to navigate change, make decisions, and take action now to create a better future.
Diversa-Leadership	Diversa-Leadership helps leaders understand people's cultural differences and leverage those differences as business strengths. Whereas the diversity of yesterday was about race and gender, the diversity of today is about cultural relativity, and so leaders must understand how different cultures think, conduct business, and consume products and services. Tomorrow's leaders will require an essential understanding of a wide variety of cultures in order to appropriately adapt business practices.
Communi-Leadership	Communi-Leadership fosters open channels of communication, dialogue, and debate among internal and external stakeholders in multiple locations. They use technology effectively across departments, locations, countries, time zones, and languages. A leader with excellent Communi-Leadership skills is considered an effective speaker and presenter in a world of diminished cues. In addition, the leader creates the climate for others to engage in ongoing effective communication.

(continued)

Figure 8-1. (continued)

Collabo-Leadership	Collabo-Leadership draws on the premise that people accomplish great things through collaborating with other talented people. For the leader, this means drawing together people with relevant abilities and varying perspectives, regardless of geographic location or culture; integrating their skills; and creating synergy. Collabo-Leadership requires leaders to genuinely know their team members, manage both vertically and horizontally, and create a zone of trust.
Edu-Leadership	Mastering Edu-Leadership may complicate everyday business operations because leaders must be prepared to develop their best talent, even if the individual moves elsewhere in the organization. Leaders must hold a dual focus on long-term goals (such as developing high potentials) and short-term goals (such as completing projects within budgets and deadlines). Sometimes, strong Edu-Leadership tailors developmental activities to the strengths and growth needs of each individual, and may entail giving up a talented team member because better developmental opportunities exist elsewhere. Ultimately, those skilled at Edu-Leadership think of creative ways to retain the best talent for their organization.

Perhaps your team has already developed the capability for some of these seven dimensions. When situations arise, individuals who possess these qualities take charge and perform. But leaders, I believe, are made—not born—so you and your team can focus on specific actions and behaviors to strengthen these dimensions. Here are seven tips for each of the seven dimensions.

Seven Tips to Sharpen Your Vista-Leadership Strategy

VISTA-LEADERSHIP
*Futurist * Visionary * Boundaryless * Strategist*

1. Imagine where you see the organization headed. At the end of each quarter, ask yourself how your actions will impact people in the next year, and then in 5, 10, 20, and even 100 years!

What future do your actions create? How will you help to shape trends in your industry?

2. Schedule regular communication with colleagues aimed at sharing information on future trends, such as new products, strategies, and business opportunities.

3. Become aware of how your organization's mission genuinely furthers your personal, regional, national, continental, and global mission. Think far out.

4. Eliminate the practices, habits, and attitudes that restrict your future vision, such as fear of irrelevance or continually engaging in linear thinking. Notice the emotional cues that cause you to stay mired in the clutter of the present so that you can better manage those emotions.

5. Blur some boundaries. Seek to resolve your problem by reading a magazine focused on a different industry, asking a friend for advice, and/or observing how a colleague in a different company addresses similar issues. A simple change in perspective can help you expand your thinking.

6. Anticipate entrepreneurial options and create a comfortable atmosphere where people feel safe to think creatively.

7. Understand the ripple effect of changes in the global market and know how they affect your business. For example, how do changes in availability and price of oil, natural gas, power, and plastic affect your company and your function? What can you do to circumvent challenges associated with depleting resources?

Seven Tips to Sharpen Your Innova-Leadership Strategy

INNOVA-LEADERSHIP
*Innovator * Creative Through Chaos * Beyond Cutting-Edge*

1. Be an informed risk taker, an abstract thinker, and someone who can remain creative through chaos. Take chances, experiment, and learn. Develop the ability to simultaneously hold

competing/conflicting ideas and remain calm in the present storm.

2. Understand how risk taking is viewed in your company's culture. What role does your network of support play in generating your innovation and risk taking? What and/or who are the forces that block creativity and change? How will you neutralize these roadblocks?

3. Actively create disruption to further the organization's advancement. Understand that innovation is not a tidy process. You must be ready to take risks even if it leads to disorder, because creativity relies on freedom. Systems destabilize when they are ready to advance.

4. Allow yourself to think unusual thoughts and to use odd processes. Talk about your ideas and exchange information with experts in your field or with someone from a different discipline. Try drawing your ideas or using words to spark free association. Analyze your ideas only when you have gotten all of them out.

5. Stimulate creativity in others; make it clear to your team that taking risks and making mistakes are allowed, as long as the mistake is acknowledged, but not repeated, and something is learned from it.

6. Informally or formally reward others for thinking of a new idea or learning something new.

7. Consider how your company's products can be adjusted to market needs, natural resources, and talent resources of a particular region or country. Remember, Innova-Leadership is about informed risk taking. The most successful risk takers are also precise, realistic, self-controlled, and logical.

Seven Tips to Sharpen Your Adapta-Leadership Strategy

ADAPTA-LEADERSHIP
*Responsive * Multidirectional * Master of Duality*

1. Learn to be a multidirectional thinker and actor; adapt at thinking various thoughts simultaneously.

2. Focus on incremental change, one experiment at a time. Break down decisions into smaller steps, and use direct and indirect feedback to adjust your next step.

3. Notice paradoxes and contradictions that create tension in your company, and harness that tension into creative solutions.

4. Understand your industry's trends around the globe. What do these global trends require for you to change? How do you want to influence these global trends?

5. Analyze and prioritize data to understand what matters and what does not; learn from experience and adjust your course accordingly.

6. Do not stay rigidly attached to your original plans and analysis if circumstances necessitate change. In today's quickly changing business environment, plans do not always occur in clear and successive steps.

7. Know how to navigate the politics of your organization. Your company is a global maze. There are indirect routes, direct routes, dead ends, turns, monotony, and a myriad of choices. How are you navigating this maze? In any organization, there are gatekeepers, idea stoppers, influencers, coaches, resisters, champions, and just plain jerks. What is your role? What do you want your role to become?

Seven Tips to Sharpen Your Diversa-Leadership Strategy

DIVERSA-LEADERSHIP

*Culturally Aware * Universal Citizen * Globally Attuned*

1. Become culturally aware of the world around you; stay globally attuned to your team's varied needs.

2. Employ various management styles to deal with multiple cultures. Adjust your management style to the needs of each individual on your team. Consider the individual's generation, location, cultural norms, strengths, and other pertinent differences.

3. Involve people from multiple backgrounds in key decision-making processes through feedback, brainstorming sessions, strategic planning, product development, and focus groups. Ensure communication channels exist that are conducive to all people contributing their strengths.

4. Be aware of language and translation barriers among you, your colleagues, vendors, investors, and customers. Have patience, be open to questions, and be willing to ask questions when you do not understand someone. Listen actively, paraphrasing what people say to show that you understand them.

5. When working with multiple cultures, eliminate disruptive habits such as using the same word often, speaking rapidly, or using judgmental words. Simplify and emphasize what you want to say. Avoid using sarcasm since some people may take it seriously.

6. Know the history and politics of the countries in which your colleagues work. Seek information from multiple sources.

7. Understand the big picture and how it relates to multiple geographical conditions. When reading your favorite newspaper, take notice of your reaction to a specific story or event. Then interpret that same story through the eyes of both a colleague and a customer in several of your company's key markets.

Seven Tips to Sharpen Your Communi-Leadership Strategy

COMMUNI-LEADERSHIP
*Transparent Performance * Continuous Communication*

1. Develop your own personal communication systems to funnel information to you. Examples include weekly virtual meetings, a quarterly on-site meeting, and as-needed phone conversations.

2.   Ask open-ended and clarifying questions. Open-ended questions probe without leading. Examples of probing questions are: "Tell me more about X," "What happened as a result of X—how did it affect you?" and "What are some possible responses to improve the situation about X?"

3.   Communication problems can run deeper than simply understanding the words and the language. Realize and be sensitive to the fact that while people may appear to understand something, they may not fully understand how to interpret it because of cultural differences.

4.   Use technology to your advantage. Technology will never replace the human element; it is simply a new medium to aid communication. Go through all of the communication channels available to you and brainstorm things that you can do to make your message more palatable and real to your audience. What medium allows you to be most yourself with colleagues in different locations? How can you take that to the next level? After you've brainstormed, ask your audience members if what you are doing works for them.

5.   Listen to people to create trust and expand possibilities. Challenge yourself to listen to everyone equally—your boss, direct reports, colleagues, and support staff. What are your listening criteria (level of education, age, rank, nationality, intelligence, skills, etc.), and do you want to expand them? What relationships can you build by listening better?

6.   Develop behaviors that invite people to clarify misunderstandings. Does your tone of voice encourage people to question, challenge, and honestly communicate with you, from answering simple yes-or-no questions to clarifying more complex concepts?

7.   Continually share information and communicate to people who need to know about your work processes, decision-making style, and concerns—wherever they are. This approach will reduce the chance of misunderstanding.

Seven Tips to Sharpen Your Collabo-Leadership Strategy

COLLABO-LEADERSHIP
*Cultivates Relationships * Facilitates Universal Wins*

1. Be a networker, an influencer, and a facilitator of relationships—encouraging the expression of opinions.

2. Create a cooperative interaction among team members by subordinating personal goals to the interest of group. Look for win-win solutions.

3. Bolster your professional network both internally and externally across divisions, business functions, ranks, tenure, and locations. Aim to establish new relationships with people of a different generation and nationality than you; connect virtually to others and nurture new and ongoing relationships.

4. As you build your network and listen to the needs and skills of the individuals in it, proactively seek to connect people in your network with each other: Give referrals and connect people who have shared interests.

5. Expand your network to creative alliances, partnerships, joint ventures, strategic alliances, and outsourcing support companies in order to access a fuller range of knowledge, skills, capabilities, and resources.

6. Let people make decisions. Do not give all the answers or tell people what to do. Understand that you can't do everything on your own. Continually organize your work and make sure that your output is always aligned with your objectives.

7. At formal meetings or in informal group conversations, practice drawing out information from others and synthesizing and reframing conflict in ways that address the needs of all parties. Do not offer your opinion or advise—allow others to come up with their own solutions first.

Seven Tips to Sharpen Your Edu-Leadership Strategy

EDU-LEADERSHIP
*Develops Global Talent * Guides Learning*

1. Provide opportunities for your direct reports; guide their career development and help them design their own performance improvement and career plan.

2. Provide regular feedback—whether acknowledging a positive outcome or correcting a performance mishap—soon after the occurrence.

3. Tailor development activities to the particular needs of your direct reports and your team, regardless of their location, position, or role. Adapt traditional practices (such as apprenticeships, employee sponsorships, group mentoring, retreats, and job rotation) to fit your group and resources.

4. Look for appropriate opportunities for you and/or your staff members to participate in projects for other departments that provide the chance to learn new skills. Offer to exchange teaching your unique skills for learning a new one.

5. Include people in your team who are more skilled in a particular area than you are. Understand that the limits to your own knowledge, skills, and functional experience limit what you can offer your direct reports; therefore, be open to connecting your subordinates to developmental opportunities outside your scope.

6. Adapt your management style to the style that your employees respond to best. Consider how the various aspects of their societal culture—law, language, politics, religious and spiritual beliefs—influence their performance and productivity.

7. Forecast the business environment in the next five to ten years. What can you do this year to develop yourself and your people for that future? What aspects of learning are going virtual?

And the Future . . .

Looking toward the future, respondents from our virtual teams study agree that VTs are here to stay, pointing to the need for a greater understanding of this work arrangement and the development of new strategies to optimize business results. According to 70 percent of respondents, virtual teams will increase in prevalence and will be considered the norm in conducting business (see Figure 8-2). According to their responses, this trend is occurring partly due to increased cost-effectiveness and the pressure of globalization. As this shift occurs, new technologies will improve the performance of virtual teams (47 percent). In addition, respondents expect that new techniques will be developed to overcome the unique challenges encountered (11 percent), as more business leaders become exposed to virtual work environments.

Increased flexibility for employees was highlighted by 9 percent of those interviewed, making virtual teams an attractive work option. In our research, we found that 4 percent of respondents believe that workers in countries such as India, Russia, and China will contribute a greater share of the global workforce. Only 2 percent of our interviewees believe that the quality of work will decrease in the virtual environment. This low statistic is reassuring as Figure 8-2 shows the trend increasing rather than stabilizing or disappearing.

Figure 8-2. The future of virtual teams.

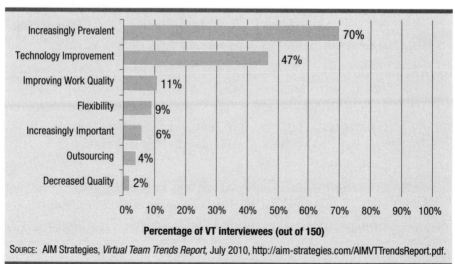

SOURCE: AIM Strategies, *Virtual Team Trends Report*, July 2010, http://aim-strategies.com/AIMVTTrendsReport.pdf.

Virtual Mindset Shift—The Next Decade

Within the next decade, the phrase *virtual mindset* will be commonplace as organizations strive to maximize their resources in a world of hypercompetition. Virtual leaders will be responsible for instilling this point of view in team members. No matter what differences in culture, national characteristics, or personal style these individuals bring to the group, they will need to adapt a worldview to effectively meet the needs of the organization. And working leaders, like you, will be front and center in making this mindset a reality as you propel your team along the virtual superhighway.

I believe that the term *virtual team* will lose its meaning as work arrangements will increasingly trend toward being partly virtual and partly on-site. As younger generations step into the workforce their lifestyles will lend themselves to flexible work arrangements, and virtual work will become an accepted norm. Advances in technology will create more options to work in more convenient places. People will need to create their own strategies to form an acceptable boundary between work and home. (We already see how being connected 24/7 has eroded boundaries between our work lives and our private lives.)

As American humorist Will Rogers noted many years ago, "Even if you're on the right track you'll get run over if you just sit there." These words are as timely now as they were almost 100 years ago, when Rogers said them. The extraordinary breadth and depth of change means that no country, organization, or person can plan on doing things the same way year after year. At the heart of this change is the complexity that makes it impossible to master what Thomas Friedman, in his book *The World Is Flat,* calls "the next layers of value creation." Global leaders responsible for virtual teams are on the front lines of these shifts. It will be up to you to master the various skills and aspects of bringing value to your organization, and that will require balancing the Seven Dimensions of GlobaLeadership.

Of course, how you choose to balance these key dimensions will also change in response to competitive forces. It is important to understand this, and to realize that each era has demanded more from its leaders than the one before. Perhaps the greatest change is that going forward, business conditions require leaders as well as teams that can bring these dimensions to life. That is actually good news, because if you and your team succeed at mastering these GlobaLeadership dimensions, you will benefit from having motivated colleagues to support and sustain your efforts.

It's Time to Refresh Your Team

Somewhere along your virtual journey you need to Refresh the team. Virtual teams are, after all, often temporary work arrangements with shifting priorities, so teams need to keep motivation high, shift gears, perform tune-ups, and refuel their energy. Figure 8-3 is a list of key points to consider when Refreshing your team.

Figure 8-3. Refreshing your team.

Step	Leader Activities
Shift Gears	• Decide if additional expertise is needed, through either training or bringing in new team members. • Be sure that onboarding activities are current. • Update equipment/technology. • Collect "lessons learned" from departing members and incorporate ideas.
Tune Up	• Reestablish norms or Rules of the Road. • Realign the team as needed. For instance, do circumstances dictate new goals? If so, are appropriate skills in place? • Tighten tire bolts by Refreshing knowledge to ensure skills. • Check in with other managers to ensure equitable workloads.
Refuel	• Encourage group activities (e.g., happy hour, team blogs). • Ask team members to recommend what works for them.

Put It in Park/Wrap Up

Many times a virtual team disbands after a project is completed. If you can, formally close this chapter of your team's experience by documenting its efforts. Review team accomplishments and contributions of individual team members. You can communicate privately with each team member or, ideally, organize a public celebration during which members socialize as well as debrief one another on their work experience.

Celebrate Success Virtually

By definition, a celebration is a commemoration that is ritualized in one's culture. National holidays, religious holidays, births and birthdays, weddings, homecomings, and the like are all types of celebrations. We humans respond positively when rewarded for our achievements, so it is no surprise that teams, whether they are on-site or dispersed, are fueled by recognition and celebration of success. Ask your team members for suggestions, or consider these small but well-received acts:

> ➤ Send a handwritten thank-you note (the personal touch is always appreciated).

> ➤ Have a senior manager congratulate the team or specific members.

> ➤ Have a team member's office decorated with a banner, a balloon, or an inexpensive gift.

On Your Way

As you come to the end of this book, I hope that you conclude, as I have, that bridging the human connection in this virtual world is your defining role. Creating collaboration and enabling leadership across the team is what leading in the twenty-first century is about. Gone are the days when staff members could be controlled through coercion and close supervision. Dispersed teams call for a new level of trust and transparency, with leaders capable of guiding them to connection and collaboration. It's up to you to create a sustainable—not situational—set of values that are rooted in the human element.

Create Presence

Leading any team is challenging enough, but leading a virtual team is a whole other world of challenges. Without the luxury of being present in person, you need to create a virtual presence. Therefore, I advise managers like you to create a *telepresence*. You need to be visible even though you are virtual. Although technology will evolve to enable better communication that more closely simulates being in the room with someone else, it will not foster the human element. That's where you come in.

Clearly, team members who have the opportunity to meet in person, at least once in a while, perform better than their virtual counterparts. I believe that you have to be physical to become virtual. When and if you do get together in person, use that precious time to focus on the things you can't do virtually. And, if you can't meet in person, then create that sense of "physical" any way you can. Recall that without the human connection there is no virtual connection.

Remember, too, that tools are no substitute for leadership, but that problems can be solved by applying appropriate tools to well-managed work practices.

Virtual teams are active social systems, and like any other social system they can be functional or dysfunctional. As you have learned in this final chapter, virtual leadership is ideally expressed through the interaction of the *entire* team, which offers a great opportunity to rethink leadership going forward. Indeed, we have much to learn about the different ways that future leadership behaviors can be expressed in emerging virtual environments. New and more sophisticated technologies are in the pipeline, ready to be adapted for your team. But it's up to you and your team members to use them productively to move business interests forward.

Welcome to the Virtual Keyboard Generation

Today's upcoming generation is the keyboard generation, and now the keyboard fits in the palm of our hand, which accounts for the ease of texting. In fact, in a given day the number of text messages far exceeds the population of the world. People are retreating more and more behind a keyboard (work and social space) instead of making real, in-person connections (in both the work and social space). It's possible to hold five simultaneous IM conversations whereas you can have only one conversation in person. I am not sure if people who communicate the former way are truly focused, although it may be productive. The question is: Have we become too enamored of technology?

As a young child visiting Disney's Future World, I was utterly fascinated by the scenario of a woman preparing a meal by issuing commands to her kitchen appliances while simultaneously talking to her husband (who appeared on a flat screen). Voice recognition systems and camera/video phones now exist, and there is no reason to doubt that more miraculous things await us.

It's possible that upcoming generations will not know what a traditional team is, as more people use technology and social networks that allow constant contact. So I ask, what else can be done to ensure that virtual teams are successful? Companies can't passively sit and wait and let things happen. They must make conscious, informed choices about what work arrangements are best. Although people can work virtually anywhere, anytime, that may not serve a particular business or unit. If companies recognize that the human connection is important, then they need to subscribe to new models. A whole generation is entering this brave new world, and its choices have yet to evolve.

Even if the future of technology is unpredictable, it is clear that virtual teams will be strongly defined by technical possibilities. Regardless of what forms these innovations take, you would be wise to follow the advice of one of my clients, a senior global director at a major electronics conglomerate: "Be simple in what you do, understand the limitation of sending a complex 'mess' over the ocean, and recognize that people are more alike than you think."

As you learned in this book, by working with practical tools and techniques, you can navigate the unique challenges faced by virtual teams. I hope you use the insights I provided to guide your exciting journey in this virtual world.

YOUR CONSOLIDATED VIRTUAL TEAM ROADMAP

From this point forward, four key elements of successful virtual teams require attention from you and your colleagues: communication, trust and accountability, conflict management, and getting deliverables out the door. Previous chapters dealt with each element individually and provided the tools and Rules of the Road to refine your direction. Now, think of this as a consolidated map to manage your virtual teams into the future.

Your final virtual team roadmap is the set of operating Rules of the Road for how your team will work together going forward.

COMMUNICATION	CONFLICT MANAGEMENT
• How will you bridge conflicting communication styles between team members? • How will you create shared understanding? • What are your expectations around how you communicate with each other? • How will you give each other feedback?	• How will you approach the major causes of conflict? • How will you handle conflict situations in the future? • How do you plan to resolve conflicting views/ideas/deadlines as a global team? • What mechanisms can be put in place to allow you to successfully negotiate conflict going forward?
TRUST AND ACCOUNTABILITY	GETTING DELIVERABLES OUT THE DOOR
• How will you create shared trust with each other? • How will you create accountability with each other? • What mechanisms are in place to engender trust within the team? • What are the two or three biggest trust builders to create trusting relationships?	• How will you coordinate quality control (QC), budget, and deadline issues with each other? • How will you set expectations regarding your part of the work product? • What are your major responsibilities to each other? • What do you hold yourself and each other accountable for?

As you look at these questions and summarize your answers, consider the following:

- How the team works as a high-performing unit to get deliverables out the door
- What team members hold themselves and each other accountable for, i.e., what members' major responsibilities are to each other

- How members create accountability
- Who depends on you, and for what
- Whom you depend on, and for what

Revisit the following specific points with your team:

Team Roadmap: Communication

1. Regularly scheduled team meetings for entire team.
   Frequency:
   Duration:
   Agenda? Yes ____ No ____ If yes, when is it distributed? _____

2. If people miss a team meeting, what process is in place to update them?

3. Submeetings for specific projects/members of the team.
   Frequency:
   Duration:
   Agenda? Yes ____ No ____ If yes, when is it distributed? _____

4. One-on-one meetings to get information/answers/resolution/clarification to problems, issues, disagreements.
   Frequency:
   Duration:
   Agenda? Yes ____ No ____ If yes, when is it distributed? _____

5. Enhancing the use of technology: intranet/team website/news bulletin board/ videoconferencing or other information-sharing mechanisms currently in place (e.g., file cabinet, team happy hour).
   Current uses:
   Potential uses:
   How often are these sharing mechanisms updated and by whom?

6. Expectations of each other.
   - How frequently will we each respond to e-mail and voice mail in a noncritical situation?
   - Is there an agreed-upon definition of a critical situation?
   - How will we convey urgency when sending a message?

- How will we let each other know when we are not available to respond immediately?
- How will we be sure understanding has occurred as a result of the communication?
- What are the consequences for not meeting expectations?

Team Roadmap: Ensuring Trust and Accountability

- Make a list of behaviors we commit to (cite specific instances):
  - What specific behaviors will we work to avoid, knowing they lead to mistrust?
  - What specific "trust builders" do we agree to put in place going forward?

Team Roadmap: Managing Conflict

- When a conflict arises, what first steps do we agree to take in order to prevent the situation from negatively impacting our work?
- If these steps do not prevent the issue from having a negative effect, what mechanisms are in place to defuse it?

Team Roadmap: Getting Deliverables out the Door

- What expectations will we put in place for each other regarding specific work responsibilities?
- What procedures can we put in place to ensure we hand off deliverables that meet QC standards and are within deadline?
- If these steps are not effective, what is our backup plan?

Reevaluating Your Team Roadmap

- Agree on your team direction for Communication, Trust and Accountability, Managing/Working Through Conflict, and Getting Deliverables out the Door.
- Every three to six months, fine-tune the plan.
- Establish a rule that any member can request a reevaluation at any time.
- Appoint a plan administrator for a six-month term. This should be a rotating position responsible for bringing new team members up to speed on the roadmap within one week of joining the team.

The Eight Characteristics of High-Performing Virtual Teams

W hy do some virtual teams function more effectively than others? Over the years, I have researched this topic and have identified certain characteristics shared by high-functioning teams. Although it would be next to impossible to assemble virtual teams that perform perfectly across all eight categories, successful virtual teams recognize the importance of creating systems and behaving consistently around these essential categories:

Category	Characteristic of Successful VTs
1. GLOBAL VS. LOCAL MINDSET	Members exhibit a global mindset whether or not they work globally. They look outward, not inward.
2. MISSION/COMMON PURPOSE	Members share responsibility for achieving the mission.
3. TRUST AND AUTHENTICITY	A culture of tolerance facilitates trust among team members.
4. MEANINGFUL COMMUNICATION	Members engage in true communication with each other. They create a shared understanding around context communication, they have access to and utilize technology to their benefit, and they engage in ongoing dialogue.

5. Flow of Information	An easy flow of information exists and is communicated using various technology mediums.
6. Conflict Management Mechanism	A conflict management mechanism is in place to process and monitor virtual conflicts that typically create misunderstanding.
7. Effective Work Systems	Work systems are in place to produce deliverables within budgetary and time constraints.
8. Positive Attitude	Team members have a positive attitude that spans time and distance challenges.

Let's take a more detailed look at the successful behaviors that describe the eight categories that anchor high-performing virtual teams.

1. Members Exhibit a Global Mindset— They Look Outward, Not Inward

We are all living in a global world, even if you're not working on a global team. With this in mind, effective virtual leaders widen their focus from the local to the global, thereby expanding the resource pool for the business. They are sensitive to the basics of working virtually—bridging cultural differences, aligning communication modes with workflow, and discouraging behaviors that exhibit territoriality. They see the big picture and make necessary accommodations to bridge potential and real differences among members. In tandem with this big-picture view is a determination to encourage diverse teammates to work outside their comfort zones and take calculated risks (which is key to bringing great ideas to the surface). Encouraging team members to develop a global mindset implicitly creates an environment of respect. Simply stated, respect engenders buy-in, without which members can't take ownership of work product and work toward a common goal.

2. Members Share Responsibility for Achieving the Mission

When team members work from the same location, personal relationships provide the glue that binds the team together. These relationships also facilitate a sense of purpose. Imbuing members with a team spirit that creates a cohesive work unit is, of course, more difficult in a virtual environment, and requires greater effort on the part of leaders to stress the commonality of purpose. High-performing teams have created the conditions where members internalize their piece of the mission, thereby transcending the isolation that defines working in a virtual environment. Furthermore, team members develop an understanding about their mutual dependence to achieve objectives.

3. A Culture of Openness Facilitates Trust and Authenticity Among Team Members

Virtual teams have a diverse membership base; the more diverse the personalities, the greater the chance for misunderstandings to arise. Effective virtual managers work to create and maintain an environment of trust to defuse miscommunications. They focus on behaviors, not on personalities, and give people the benefit of the doubt, because they know this engenders trust. When members know that they will not be penalized for asking basic questions or for proposing "wrong" solutions, they are more willing to contribute their ideas and engage in breakthrough thinking. As the saying goes, none of us is as smart as all of us.

When a zone of trust is created, successful global leaders are authentic. They "say what they mean and mean what they say" to a high degree and model the behavior for their team members. They can be counted on to follow through on what they promise; talk and action are aligned. Being able to take people at their word increases the likelihood that the team functions at a high capacity and that valuable time is not wasted revisiting tasks and issues that were previously addressed.

4. Members Engage in Meaningful Communication with Each Other

First and foremost, high-performing virtual teams (1) establish and maintain standards on frequency and modes of communication and (2) hold members accountable for acting accordingly. Members make sure they are available to the team according to the established standards that everyone signed off on. For example, everyone knows the team's normal working hours and how often members check voice mail, e-mail, and interoffice mail. They know how quickly to respond to or acknowledge each type of communication. In high-performing virtual teams, the message sender takes responsibility for prioritizing communication, clearly indicating what is informational and what requires action, and by whom.

Team members have figured out how to compensate for the loss of physical context in a virtual environment and make a real effort to share an understanding of situations that arise; they are willing to communicate and work together to find solutions. In addition, they are proficient at distance communication, and yet regularly use synchronous communication at critical points to speak with each other.

5. An Easy Flow of Information Exists and Is Communicated Using Various Forms of Technology

Information is the lifeblood of projects, and effective global managers have processes in place to ensure that all stakeholders are comfortable in asking for what they need, and stating when their needs are not met. In addition, everyone has access to appropriate technology to enable reliable, current exchange of information. Of critical importance is the team's access to competent and timely technical support, including the assurance that file sharing and exchange is not compromised by compatibility issues.

Data comes at members of virtual teams at a relentless pace. If information is "pushed" to us (through unfiltered e-mails, phone calls, and the like), then our time is not our own. Pulled information, which is available through e-bulletin boards, intranets, and, again, e-mail, offers greater control because we choose when to take in information. In high-performing global teams, the ratio of pushed to pulled information is lower than normal.

6. A Conflict Management Mechanism Is in Place

Conflicts are inevitable in the virtual environment where decision makers believe strongly in their own points of view and cannot hash out issues face-to-face. Furthermore, simple miscommunications often don't get acknowledged and fixed, and trust gets eroded. In virtual environments a conflict can be swept under the rug until it becomes such a big issue that it is hard to ignore. Effectively managed global teams have systems to resolve the tensions that arise from legitimate issues, so energy can be used productively, instead of being turned against team members. Conflicts are identified early on and dealt with fairly, in the knowledge that a well-managed conflict clears the way for increased team commitment. Here again, the manager actively engages team members in communicating issues (no issue is too minor if someone brings it up) and follows up to ensure appropriate resolution. When a culture of conflict management is in place, members more easily communicate one-on-one, thereby avoiding lengthy, energy-draining confrontations.

7. Work Systems Produce Deliverables Within Budgetary and Time Constraints

There is no substitute for operational competence in a global marketplace. When team members are geographically dispersed, a rigorous effort is required to coordinate and align components of critical work systems to meet deadlines within time and budgetary constraints. High-performing teams have figured out how operational nuts and bolts fit together to get deliverables out the door as efficiently and cost-effectively as possible.

8. Members Have a Positive Attitude That Spans Time and Distance Challenges

With an understanding that a positive, "can do" attitude stimulates productivity, members of high-functioning virtual teams assume their efforts will lead to success. When conflicts and tension arise, as they inevitably do, members hold these situations within the context of the larger picture and look to quickly find solutions, rather than assign blame. Global leaders stress the need for members to give each other the benefit of the doubt when frustrating situations come up, and to "walk a mile" in the other person's shoes to gain an understanding of another's point of view.

Index